GOD, WHAT'S YOUR NAME?

KAY ARTHUR
JANNA ARNDT

HARVEST HOUSE™ PUBLISHERS

EUGENE, OREGON

Illustrations by Steve Bjorkman

Cover by Left Coast Design, Portland, Oregon

DISCOVER 4 YOURSELF is a registered trademark of The Hawkins Children's LLC. Harvest House Publishers, Inc., is the exclusive licensee of the federally registered trademark DISCOVER 4 YOURSELF.

Discover 4 Yourself® Inductive Bible Studies for Kids
GOD, WHAT'S YOUR NAME?
Copyright © 2003 by Precept Ministries International
Published by Harvest House Publishers
Eugene, Oregon 97402
www.harvesthousepublishers.com

ISBN-13: 978-0-7369-1161-0
ISBN-10: 0-7369-1161-8

Printed in the United States of America

08 09 10 11 12 13 / ML-MS / 12 11 10 9 8 7 6

For the Kids

Your boundless enthusiasm and unending questions
brighten my day and encourage me as I watch you grow in God's
Word. Teaching you is one of my greatest blessings!
May you know your God so you can display
strength and take action—Daniel 11:32.

I love each and every one of you.
Miss Janna
(also known as Mrs. Arndt)

CONTENTS

Spying Out Truth—
A Bible Study *You* Can Do!

SPYING OUT TRUTH—
A BIBLE STUDY YOU CAN DO!

Pssssst! Over here. Code word? Good! Now press the hidden lever under the root of the tree and climb on up. It's great to have you back at the tree house. Did you recognize us with our cool disguises? Molly, Sam (the great detective beagle), and I want to recruit you to help us spy out truth and become secret agents for God. Doesn't that sound exciting? By the way, my name is Max. Are you ready to join us in an exciting adventure in God's Word as we become God's secret agents and take on the mission of discovering WHO God is and WHAT His different aliases are? (*Aliases* are the other names that God goes by.)

"Did you know that God has many different names in the Bible? These names describe God's character and show us just WHO He really is. WHAT are those different names? WHAT will we discover about God as we uncover each name?

"You have so much to discover about God as you go undercover to spy out truth by studying the Bible—God's Operations Manual, the source of all truth—and by asking God's Spirit to lead and guide you. You also have this book, your codebook, which is an inductive Bible study. That word *inductive* means you go straight to the Bible *yourself* to investigate what God's Word says and discover what it means, instead of depending on what someone else says it means.

"So grab your disguises and check out the list of things you will need to get started! Your mission, should you decide to accept it, is to find out just WHO God is by discovering His different code names and finding out WHAT these names mean so that you can know your God, display strength, and take action (Daniel 11:32).

"Are you ready? Great! See you at the PMP (Personal Meeting Point) at 0800 hours."

THINGS YOU'LL NEED
▼

NEW AMERICAN STANDARD BIBLE
(UPDATED EDITION)—OR, PREFERABLY,
THE NEW INDUCTIVE STUDY BIBLE
(NISB)
PEN OR PENCIL
COLORED PENCILS
INDEX CARDS
A DICTIONARY
THIS WORKBOOK

A SPECIAL MISSION— OPERATION KGN (KNOWING GOD'S NAME)

"Good, you made it to the PMP. Molly and I are so excited that you have accepted this mission to become a secret agent for God! Aren't you thrilled about being recruited for this special mission of discovering WHO God is?

"We have someone we want you to meet: our Uncle Matt. He is a secret agent for the CIA. Uncle Matt is excited that we really want to know who God is, so he has recruited us along with two of our friends, Colby and Ruthi, to become secret agents for God. Uncle Matt is going to be our trainer as he teaches us all about spying. And don't forget to keep your eyes out for 'you know who'—our secret weapon. You guessed it: Sam. He is already sniffing out clues for this secret mission.

"To become God's secret agent and be able to serve and love Him with all your heart, soul, and mind, you have to know WHO God is and HOW He operates. If you don't really know God, how can you have a relationship with Him and serve as one of His special agents?

"Are you ready to get started on your field training so you can earn your secret agent badge of service and be deployed on God's mission field to be used for His service? Great! Then let's get started."

FOR YOUR EYES ONLY—
HOW DO YOU SEE GOD?

"OK," Uncle Matt said as we gathered around the table at our PMP—Uncle Matt's summer cabin. "I have a top secret notebook for each one of you to go with your Operations Manual. As we open up our Operations Manual, the Bible, to begin our field training, WHAT is the first thing you need to do? Do you know? That's right! Pray. Bible study should always begin with prayer. We need to ask God, our Commander in Chief, to direct us and teach us by His Spirit as we begin our top priority mission in His Word. This will help us understand what He says and make sure we handle His Word accurately. Let's pray, and then we can get started on our mission."

Your first field training assignment is to describe God on the lines below. Take a few minutes and think about WHO God is to you. Write down the words that come to your mind as you think about God. Do you think of God as loving or as a judge? Is He a friend or a dictator? It's important that you examine how you see God because the way you see God affects your relationship with Him. Our mission is to discover WHO God really is, not WHO we think He is.

So take a few minutes and describe what you think about God in your notebook below.

TOP SECRET—FOR YOUR EYES ONLY

_____

_____

_____

_____

Great! As we continue our training, ask yourself, "When I have a problem or something bad happens to me, what do I do? Do I run to my room? Do I go to my mom and dad to talk? Do I talk to my friends? WHAT do I do when I am afraid or worried? WHERE do I go for help?"

"Where should you run in times of trouble? Do you know?" Uncle Matt asked Max, Molly, Ruthi, and Colby as they sat around the table inside the cabin. "You may already know the answer, but I want you to discover it for yourself straight from God's Word, our Operations Manual. I have planted a coded message outside at one of the secret places that I told you would make a good drop point. This message is the first clue in our mission. You need to find it, bring it inside, and decode it so you can see where you need to run in times of trouble. All right, GSAs (God's secret agents), let's do it!"

"Let's race," yelled Molly as they ran out the door. "Ruthi and I will work together as a team to see which team can find it first!"

"You're on!" yelled Colby as he jumped off the front porch of Uncle Matt's cabin. "Let's go, Max!"

"We found it, Uncle Matt!" Max exclaimed as he burst through the cabin door.

"Great!" replied Uncle Matt. "Now decode the message by looking at the Box and Dot Secret Code in your codebook on page 10. Write the answer on the lines underneath the secret message. This will also be your first memory verse in your field training.

"One of the requirements to become a secret agent for God is to develop your skills of memorization. You never know when you may have to memorize secret documents out in the field. You will receive a new verse each week to help develop these memorization skills. Part of your training requires that you practice saying these verses three times in a row three times a day until you have them down.

"Get started, GSAs. Decode your first memory verse."

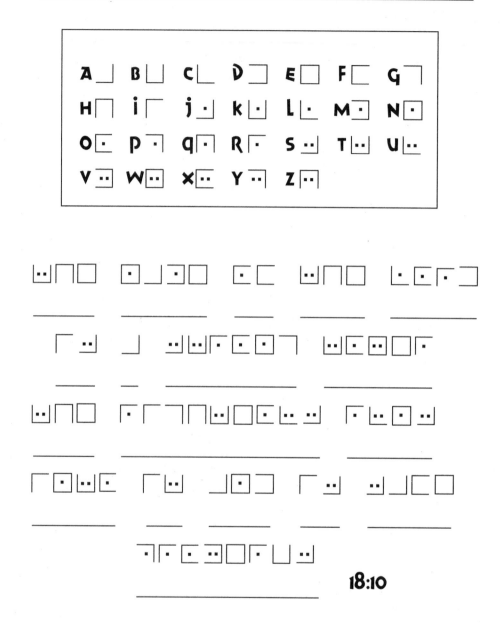

18:10

All right, you have cracked your first code! Now WHAT do we learn from this verse? Secret agents need to be able to evaluate and analyze all the information that they have collected. They need great observation skills.

Let's get started gathering our intel (that means the intelligence, the secret information). Let's ask the 5 W's and an H questions. What are the 5 W's and an H? They are the WHO, WHAT, WHERE, WHEN, WHY, and HOW questions.

1. Asking WHO helps you find out:

    WHO wrote this?

    WHOM are we reading about?

    To WHOM was it written?

    WHO said this or did that?

2. WHAT helps you understand:

    WHAT is the author talking about?

    WHAT are the main things that happen?

3. WHERE helps you learn:

    WHERE did something happen?

    WHERE did they go?

    WHERE was this said?

    When we discover a "WHERE" we double-underline the WHERE in green.

4. WHEN tells us about time. We mark it with a green clock like this: 🕐

    WHEN tells us:

    WHEN did this event happen or WHEN will it happen?

    WHEN did the main characters do something? It helps us to follow the order of events.

5. WHY asks questions like:

    WHY did he say that?

WHY did they go there?

WHY did this happen?

6. HOW lets you figure out things like:

HOW is something to be done?

HOW did people know something had happened?

Now gather the intel from our memory verse on page 10.

Proverbs 18:10 WHAT is our strong tower?

_____

HOW are the righteous safe?

_____

Now read Psalm 20:7 printed out below.

Some boast in chariots and some in horses, but we will boast in the name of the LORD, our God.

Psalm 20:7 WHAT are we to boast in?

_____

Do you know what it means "to boast in"? "To boast in" means "to have confidence in," "to trust in." That means you can believe God. In biblical times a name represented a person's character. God's name represents His character, His attributes (qualities or characteristics that belong to Him), and His nature. To know God's name is to know God. We trust Him to be everything He says He is, to not change. When we boast in His name, it means we have confidence in WHO God is!

WHY would some people boast (put their trust) in chariots and horses? Do you know? In Old Testament days, chariots and horses were means of protection and escape, like tanks or armored vehicles would be today. So these people put their confidence in chariots and horses as a way to protect themselves and help them escape. But we have already seen where we are to put our confidence. Write it out one more time. In WHOM are we to boast? WHERE do we put our trust?

_____

Let's read Psalm 50:14,15 printed out below.

> **14** Offer to God a sacrifice of thanksgiving and pay your vows to the Most High; **15** Call upon Me in the day of trouble; I shall rescue you, and you will honor Me.

Psalm 50:15 WHAT are we to do in the day of trouble?

_____

Psalm 50:14 WHO is this "Me" in verse 15? Look at verse 14 to help you see WHO the "Me" is.

_____

Psalm 50:15 WHAT will God do when we call upon Him?

_____

WHAT will we do? _____

Now let's look at one last verse: Psalm 124:8.

> *Our help is in the name of the L*ORD*, who made heaven and earth.*

Psalm 124:8 WHERE is our help?

_____

Since we know that God's name shows us His character—WHO He is—WHAT do we learn about God in
Psalm 124:8?

_____

Way to go! You have just uncovered some very important
intel. Remember, intel is the intelligence, the secret information, on WHO or WHAT you are investigating. WHAT intel
did you discover about God? You now know that God is to be
your Protector and your way of escape. Have you ever
thought of God as your Protector before today? You are to run
to Him in times of trouble, and He will rescue you!

Isn't it awesome to see that God loves you and will rescue
you when hard times come? Our help is in God's name. God's
name is a strong tower. When you call on His name, you will
be safe. As we finish our training for the day, draw a picture
of a strong tower in the box below to help you remember that
God's name is a strong tower. It is powerful. It will protect
you and keep you safe!

Now let's head back to the tree house. Tomorrow we will
continue our mission of discovering God's names.

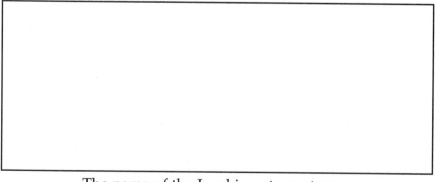

The name of the Lord is a strong tower

UNCOVERING GOD'S PROMISES

"Come in Mike-Oscar-Lima-Lima-Yankee," Max called out as he radioed Molly on the walkie-talkie.

"Roger, Mike-Alpha-X-ray," Molly replied. "Continue. Over."

"Roger. Colby and Ruthi have arrived. We are ready to head back to our PMP. What's your location? Over."

"A minute away from the tree house. Over."

"Wilco. Out," Max replied as he finished his radio transmission to Molly and turned to Colby and Ruthi. "Molly will be here in a minute. Then we can head back to Uncle Matt's cabin. Today Uncle Matt wants us to practice our bike patrol skills as we ride to the cabin to make sure that the area is secure. Are you ready? Do you have your walkie-talkies?"

"We sure are!" both Ruthi and Colby exclaimed.

"Hey, let's grab our sunglasses and surprise Molly when she gets here from behind the tree house," Ruthi suggested.

"Too late," Molly said as Ruthi finished her suggestion.

"Hey, how did you get in without us hearing you?" Colby asked.

"Isn't that part of being a secret agent—slipping in without being noticed?"

"Good work, Molly," Max said. "Now let's grab those sunglasses and our bikes. We need to do our bike patrol around the lake just like the CIA does around the White House to keep it secure."

"Let's go," Molly said as they climbed down the tree house ladder and flipped the lever for the secret door. "We are on our way!"

Now that you have patrolled the

lake and slipped into Uncle Matt's cabin, it's time to pull out your Operations Manual. But what's the first thing you need to do, secret agent? Pray! Way to go! Now you're ready.

"Hey, guys," Uncle Matt said as he walked into the room, "that was a very good approach to the cabin. Let's get ready for your next assignment. Yesterday, you took a look at one verse from Psalm 20. Today we are going to look at the whole psalm and gather more intel to see what we can discover about the Lord's promises to us."

Today as we read Psalm 20, we need to mark some key words.

What are *key words?* Key words are words that pop up more than once. They are called *key words* because they help unlock the meaning of the chapter or book that you are studying and give you clues about what is most important in a passage of Scripture.

- Key words are usually used over and over again.

- Key words are important.

- Key words are used by the writer for a reason.

Once you discover a key word, you need to mark it in a special way using a special color or symbol so that you can immediately spot it in Scripture. Don't forget to mark any pronouns that go with the key words, too! WHAT are pronouns? Check out Max and Molly's notes below.

PRONOUNS

Pronouns are words that take the place of nouns. A noun is a person, place, or thing. A pronoun stands in for a noun! Here's an example: "Molly and Max are spying out truth in God's Word. They can't wait to discover some of God's aliases." The word *they* is a pronoun because it takes the place of Molly's and Max's names in the second sentence. It is another word we use to refer to Molly and Max.

Watch for these pronouns when you are marking key words:

I	you	he	she
me	yours	him	her
mine		his	hers
we	it	they	
our	its	them	
ours		their	

Let's get started. Read Psalm 20 printed out below and mark the following key words:

Lord (God, King) (draw a purple triangle and color it yellow)

name (color it orange)

trouble, need, or help (put a blue cloud around it)

Psalm 20

1 May the LORD answer you in the day of trouble! May the name of the God of Jacob set you securely on high! **2** May He send you help from the sanctuary and support you from Zion! **3** May He remember all your meal offerings and find your burnt offering acceptable! Selah. **4** May He grant you your heart's desire and fulfill all your counsel! **5** We will sing for joy over your victory, and in the name of our God we will set up our banners. May the LORD fulfill all your petitions. **6** Now I know that the LORD saves His anointed; He will answer him from His holy heaven with the saving strength of His right hand. **7** Some boast in chariots and some in horses, but we will boast in the name of the LORD, our God. **8** They have bowed down and fallen, but we have risen and stood upright. **9** Save, O LORD; may the King answer us in the day we call.

Now let's make a list of the promises of the Lord from Psalm 20.

Psalm 20:1 May the LORD _____ you in the day of_____. May the _____ of the God of Jacob_____ you _____ on _____.

Psalm 20:2 May He send you _____ from the sanctuary and_____ you from Zion!

Psalm 20:3 May He remember all your _____ _____ and find your _____ _____ acceptable!

Psalm 20:4 May He grant you your _____ _____ and fulfill all your _____!

Psalm 20:5 May the LORD fulfill all your_____.

Psalm 20:6 The LORD saves His _____; He will _____ him from His holy heaven.

Psalm 20:9 May the King _____ us in the day we _____.

Great! Now gather the intel. Ask the 5 W's and an H questions.

Psalm 20:6 WHOM does God save?

_____

Psalm 20:1 WHAT sets a person securely on high?

_____

Psalm 20:5 HOW do we set up our banners?

_____

WHAT are we singing for joy over? WHAT has the name of the Lord given us?

Our v _ _ _ _ _ y

Psalm 20:7,8 WHY are they boasting in the name of the Lord?

Because they have _____ and stood

_____

Psalm 20:8 WHAT happened to those who trusted in chariots and horses?

They have _____ down and _____.

Do you see the difference between those whose trust is in the Lord and those who have put their trust in horses and chariots? The difference is between standing and falling down! Isn't it amazing to see all that the Lord promises to those who belong to Him?

Did you notice how powerful God's name is? It's what sets you securely on high. Being set securely on high is like being placed up high on a rock where you are inaccessible, out of the reach of danger. You are protected! God's name is your victory, your confidence, and your salvation.

Aren't you excited about uncovering God's names after all you have seen today? Just imagine what knowing God's name is going to mean to your life!

Now as we head outside to do our PT—physical training (secret agents have to be in top-notch physical condition)—practice saying your memory verse three times in a row as you climb those ropes and move through Uncle Matt's obstacle course. Tomorrow we will continue our special operation—KGN (Knowing God's Name).

BREAKING THE CODE—WHO IS GOD?

"Hey, guys, look at this," Max exclaimed as he opened the package he discovered at the tree house's secret drop site. "It's a CD from Uncle Matt."

"Cool," replied Colby. "Let's play it."

"OK," Max replied as he put the CD into the CD player and hit the Play button.

As the CD started to play, the kids recognized Uncle Matt's voice. "Attention, GSAs! You have been selected to recover the first secret code that will reveal one of God's names and His character. If you decide to accept this mission, then you need to head to the park to look for a man wearing purple-and-yellow striped pants and a funny-looking hat.

"Once you have spotted your contact, have Ruthi approach him. He is looking for a redhead wearing red. She needs to ask him for a blue balloon shaped like a crescent moon. It will be your job to figure out where the secret code is located and bring this code to the cabin to be decoded. See you at the lake."

"Wow! This is so cool," squealed Molly. "I wonder how Uncle Matt knew Ruthi would be wearing red."

"He's a secret agent, Molly," Max replied. "His eyes are everywhere!"

Everyone cracked up laughing at Max. "Well, GSAs, are you ready to hit the park?"

"Yeah!" Molly, Ruthi, and Colby all yelled as Sam barked in agreement and wagged his tail.

"Then let's get on our bikes and head to the park. But first we need to pray for a successful mission and ask for God's direction and protection," Max said.

After Max led the GSA team in prayer, they headed to the park to discover their contact, the man in purple-and-yellow striped pants and a funny-looking hat.

"Look over there!" Ruthi cried out. "See that clown with the balloons? He has on purple-and-yellow striped pants and a funny-looking hat."

"All right," Max replied. "Go make contact, and we will back you up from that park bench."

As Ruthi approached the clown, she asked him, "Sir, do you have a blue balloon shaped like a crescent moon?"

"I sure do," he replied. "That will be one dollar."

Ruthi paid the clown, and he handed her the blue balloon.

"Now what do we do?" Molly asked as Ruthi came back to the bench with the balloon. "He gave Ruthi the balloon, but where's the secret code?"

Just then, Sam started barking and jumping, trying to snap at the balloon as it bobbed up and down on the string. "Stop it, Sam!" Max scolded just as Sam nipped the balloon with his teeth and the balloon made a loud pop!

"Look!" exclaimed Colby. "A piece of paper fell out of the balloon."

Max picked up the piece of paper and opened it to discover some mixed-up letters typed out. "I can't believe it! Sam, you have done it again. You have discovered our secret code! Let's get on our bikes and head straight to the lake. We need to decode this message to discover God's name."

"Great work, GSAs," Uncle Matt said as the kids flew off their bikes and Max handed him the message.

Max laughed. "We didn't figure it out, Uncle Matt. Sam did!"

"Well, Sam, it looks like you are going to be the first to earn your secret service badge," Uncle Matt replied as he patted Sam's head.

"Now you need to get to work, GSAs. Use the secret

code from your codebook to crack this code and discover God's name."

To decode this secret message, GSAs, all you need to do is look at the first letter in the secret message, which is the letter *F*. Now look at the alphabet code below. What letter comes before the letter *F* in the alphabet? *E*, that's right. So on the line under the secret code write the letter *E* under the letter *F* in your message.

Now continue doing the same thing for each of the letters in the secret message. Choose the letter of the alphabet that comes before the letter that is written in code to finish decoding your message.

FMPIJN

ALPHABET CODE

A B C D E F G H I J K L M N O P Q R S T U
V W X Y Z

You did it! You just discovered the first name of God used in the Bible in Genesis 1:1. This name for God is a Hebrew word, because the Old Testament, where Genesis is found, was written in Hebrew.

What does this word *Elohim* mean? This word designates God as God. It means "to fear" or "to reverence." The first part of the word, *El*, means "mighty" or "strong." It is the word we use to refer to Almighty God. The *im* ending is very important because it is a plural ending.

Now look up and read Genesis 1:1 in your Operations Manual, the Bible, to discover the first time we see this name *Elohim* for God (pronounced like this: *el-oh-HEEM*).

Now evaluate the intel.

Genesis 1: 1 WHOM do we see in the beginning?

WHAT is God doing in this passage?

_____

WHAT does this show us about God? To find out, look at the same alphabet code that you just used and decode the message below.

HPE   JT   PVS   DSFBUPS

____   ____   ____   _____

Elohim is the word for God as Creator in Genesis 1:1. The fact that this name for God has a plural ending tells us a secret right from the beginning about God. Let's see if we can find out WHAT that secret is.

First let's look up and read Genesis 1:2.

WHO was moving over the surface of the waters?

_____

That's the Holy Spirit! Isn't it amazing? We have just seen that both God and the Holy Spirit had a part in Creation. Was there anyone else there when God created the earth in the beginning? Let's do some cross-referencing to find out.

WHAT is cross-referencing? Cross-referencing is comparing Scripture with Scripture by going to other passages in the Bible. This is a very important Bible study tool that we can use as we search out the meaning of Scripture, because we know that Scripture never contradicts Scripture.

We also have to remember to keep an eye out for context as we look at other passages. WHAT is context? Context is the setting in which something is found. This is very important in Bible study. Context is a combination of two words: *con*, which means "with," and *text*, which means "what is written."

So when you look for context in the Bible, you look at the verses surrounding the passage you are studying. Then you also think about where the passage fits in the big picture of the chapter and book you are studying, and then how it fits into the whole Bible.

Now that we know about cross-referencing and context, let's look up and read John 1:1-3,14.

John 1:1 WHO was in the beginning?_____

Let's list what we see about the Word in John 1:1:

a. The Word was in the _____.

b. The Word _____ _____ God.

c. The Word was _____.

Hmmmm. Isn't that interesting? The Word not only was with God, but the Word also was God.

So HOW many are claiming to be God?_____

What do you think that means? Could it mean that the Word was not only God, but also someone else? Let's find out.

John 1:2 WHO was in the beginning with God?_____

WHO is this "He"? Read John 1:14.

WHO became flesh and dwelt among us? WHO is the only begotten from the Father? WHO is God's Son?

_____

John 1:3 HOW did all things come into being?

_____

And WHO did we discover in John 1:14 was this "Him"?

_____

Look up and read Hebrews 1:2. Through WHOM was the world made?

_____

Look up and read Colossians 1:16. WHO is the "Him" that all things have been created through and for? Look at the context in verses 13-15. WHO is God's beloved Son?

_____

By looking at all these different verses, we can see that in the beginning Elohim—God the Father; God the Son, Jesus; and God the Holy Spirit—each had a part in Creation. Isn't that *awesome?*

Now look up and read Genesis 1:26,27.

Do you know WHO the "Us" is in this passage? Name the "Us."

WHO are the three we discovered who each had a part in Creation?

_____

Genesis 1:26 WHOM did God create in this verse?

_____

HOW was man created?

_____

You were created in the image of God. *Amazing!* You have just uncovered a very important characteristic about God. He is the Creator. He created the heavens and the earth, the sun, moon, stars, dry land, seas, the plants, and animals. And most importantly, God created you!

Look up and read Genesis 1:31.

WHAT did God see about all that He had made?

That it was _____ _____

Have you ever had kids tease you about the way you look? _____

WHAT did they tease you about? Was it your height, freckles, weight, nose, or something else? Write it out below.

_____

HOW did it make you feel: hurt, sad, or mad?

_____

Have you ever teased someone else about the way God made them? _____

HOW do you think it made them feel?

_____

HOW do you think God feels when you do that since He created them? _____

Think about this the next time you start to make fun of someone or someone makes fun of you. WHO made you just the way you are?_____ No matter how imperfect you think you are, or what anyone else says about you, you need to remember that God is the Creator. He looked at all He had created, and according to Him, everything He made, including you, was very good!

Now look at Exodus 4:10 printed below.

> **10** Then Moses said to the LORD, "Please, Lord, I have never been eloquent, neither recently nor in time past, nor since You have spoken to Your

servant; for I am slow of speech and slow of tongue." **11** The LORD said to him, "Who has made man's mouth? Or who makes him mute or deaf, or seeing or blind? Is it not I, the LORD?"

Exodus 4:11 WHO made man's mouth? Who made man mute, or deaf, or seeing, or blind?

_____

Now look up and read John 9:1-3.

John 9:3 WHY was the man born blind?

_____

God has a purpose for the way He made you. God has a purpose for everything He does! God our Creator makes us exactly the way He wants us to be and sees it as very good! *Amazing!*

Do you ever complain about how you look or what your gifts and abilities are? _____

Should you complain, if God created you in His image the way He wanted you to be? Think about it. We will discover more about our Creator tomorrow. Now as you take Sam for a run around the lake, don't forget to practice your memory verse!

A SPECIAL IDENTITY — GOD CREATED YOU!

"How do you like this disguise?" Molly asked Max, Colby, and Ruthi as she held up part of the costume she was working on.

"Pretty cool," Ruthi replied.

"I love learning how to be a spy," Max joined in. "Making these disguises and pretending to be different people sure is a lot of fun."

"It sure is," Molly added. "But don't forget what we learned yesterday. God created us to be just like He wanted us to be, zits and all!"

"Yeah," Colby laughed, "but who wants to have any zits?"

Everyone cracked up laughing at Colby's comment, and Ruthi added, "No one does, but God wants us to accept ourselves just the way He made us, with no complaining, especially since zits are just a part of growing up!"

"I know. I know. I was just kidding!" Colby replied.

"OK, guys," Max said, "it's about time to put away our disguises and pull out our Operations Manual to see what else we can discover about our Creator. Why don't you lead us in prayer this time, Molly? Then we can get started spying out God's truth."

Yesterday we uncovered our first clue to God's character. We saw that God's name shows us He is the Creator of everything, including us! We also saw that God creates us just the way He wants us to be. There are no accidents or mistakes. God is the One who makes man mute (that means someone who can't talk), deaf, seeing, blind, or whatever it is that makes someone physically different from other people.

Today we are going to take a closer look at HOW God created us and discover our purpose on this earth. Have you ever wondered WHY you were born or WHY you are here on earth? Guess what—today you are going to discover the answers to those questions. You are going to see WHY God created you!

First let's take a closer look at HOW God created us. Let's look at our Observation Worksheet on Psalm 139. Observation Worksheets are pages that have the Bible text printed out for you to use as you do your research on knowing God's names. So turn to page 166 and read Psalm 139.

Now, GSAs, let's gather the intel for our special mission.

Psalm 139:1-4 WHO knows you? WHO knows when you sit down or stand up? WHO is intimately acquainted with all your ways? WHO knows it all?

_____

Psalm 139:13 WHO formed your inward parts? _____

HOW were you made?

_____

Did you know that you are a Designer's creation? You are completely designed by the hand of God!

Psalm 139:14 WHAT are you to do?

_____

WHY? HOW are you made?

_____

WHAT are God's works? _____

Psalm 139:15 Was your frame hidden from God? _____

Psalm 139:16 WHAT did God write in His book?

_____

Wow! Isn't this *incredible?* When you grab hold of the fact that God is your Creator, it will change how you see everything! The Creator of the universe formed you in your mother's womb! Nothing was hidden from God. He made you exactly the way He wanted you to be, and you are to give thanks to Him!

Do you do that? Are you thankful for the way God made you, or do you gripe and complain? Do you feel like a misfit, a mistake, or an accident? If you do, then you have believed a lie, because God shows you right in His Word that He is the Creator and no one else. There are no mistakes. He forms us and weaves us. We are fearfully and wonderfully made. God Himself ordains all of our days! God has individually and specifically created you to be you! You are special. You have worth and value no matter what the world or anyone else tells you!

Now let's discover the WHY. WHY did God create you? Look at your Observation Worksheet for Isaiah 43 on page 167.

Read Isaiah 43:1-7.

Isaiah 43:1 HOW does God call us? _____

WHO are we to God? "You are _____!"

Isaiah 43:2 WHAT will happen when we pass through the waters?

_____

Isaiah 43:4 WHAT are we in God's sight?

_____

HOW does God feel about us?

_____

Isaiah 43:7 WHY did God create us?

_____

WHAT does it mean to be created for God's glory? That means we should live to bring God honor. We are to live in a way that gives all of creation a correct opinion of who God is. We should not complain about who we are or how we are made, because we know that God has a purpose in creating us this way. Our actions and who we are should show other people just WHO God is.

We are to show the world the character of God. We need to do the things that God wants us to do, such as becoming like Christ, loving other people as ourselves, forgiving others when they hurt us, using our gifts and talents, and telling people about Jesus.

Look at John 17:4 printed out below.

> *I glorified You on the earth, having accomplished the work which You have given Me to do.*

This "I" that is speaking is Jesus. HOW did Jesus glorify God on the earth?

_____

HOW about you? WHAT is the work God has for you to do? WHAT are your gifts and talents that God has given you?

_____

Are you using those gifts for His glory? Are you doing the things that God wants you to do, such as:

• Loving other people? Are you kind to everyone or just to your friends? Do you befriend the kids who are left out? Tell what you do on the line below.

_____

• Do you witness to kids who don't know Jesus? _____

• Do you give God the credit for your abilities, or do you brag about your accomplishments?

_____

- Do you do anything that doesn't bring God glory, such as making fun of someone at school? Do you laugh at him and talk about him behind his back?
  ____ Yes ____ No

Let's look at one more verse that tells you why you were born.

> *Worthy are You, our Lord and our God, to receive glory and honor and power; for You created all things, and because of Your will they existed, and were created* (Revelation 4:11).

Revelation 4:11 WHY were you born? WHY do You exist? Because of God's _____.

Isn't that awesome? You were created for God's will. Your life is to be lived to show the world God's character: His love, His mercy, His peace, His gentleness, His forgiveness. You are to live for God to accomplish His will.

You were not an accident. God planned your birth and numbered your days. He loves you. You are precious in His sight. He has called you by name. You are His!

Now take a picture of yourself and glue it in the space below.

Think about the ways that God has created you. HOW are you special? Are you good in math? Do you like to make up stories? Can you sing? Are you good at sports? Would you rather play the piano, read a good book, or study nature?

Write a note to God on the lines below and tell Him how you feel about yourself. Tell God what you wish you could change, and then tell Him you will accept the things you cannot change because you know He made you for His special purpose. Thank God for the special gifts and abilities He gave you.

_____

_____

_____

_____

Fantastic! Now ask God, your Elohim, to help you live for His glory and His purpose. Remember, you have a special identity. You are created in the image of God. He loves you!

VANQUISH FEAR BY DISCOVERING GOD'S NAME

It's great to have you back at the lake! Now that you have discovered the first name used for God in the Bible, are you ready for your next mission? Today Uncle Matt has made a drop somewhere around the lake that will help us discover another one of God's names. Your mission, GSA, is to scout around the lake for the next secret message that will reveal God's name.

Have you prayed? Great! Now let's get started. Uncle Matt rubbed one of Sam's special treats over the envelope so that Sam can put us on the right trail by sniffing out our next clue.

"Come on, Sam," Max called out. "Let's go, boy! It's time to go out into the open and recover the next clue." Max let Sam loose as he barked his agreement and started running around, sniffing every leaf and bush.

"Oh no, Max, do you think he has the scent? Look at him! He's sniffing everything in sight," Molly cried out.

About that time Colby yelled out, "Look, he's headed toward the lake! Looks like he's finally caught the scent."

OK, GSAs, grab your sunglasses and follow Sam!

You did it! Sam put you on the trail, and you found the next secret message buried under the big rock next to the dock. Now head to the cabin and crack the code by using the inverse alphabet in your codebook.

Here's the message:

VO   VOBLM
____   _____

To decode this message, use the Inverse Alphabet Code below to find the letter of the alphabet that represents the letter written in the message. The first letter in our secret message is the letter *V*. Look at the inverse alphabet under the letter *V* and write out the letter that is representing the letter *V*, which would be the letter *E*. Now write the letter *E* on the line under the secret message. Then do the same thing for the rest of the letters, until you have uncovered God's name.

INVERSE ALPHABET CODE

A B C D E F G H I J K L M N O P Q R S T U V W X Y Z
Z Y X W V U T S R Q P O N M L K J I H G F E D C B A

Mission accomplished! Another name of God is revealed! WHAT does this Hebrew name *El Elyon* (pronounced *el el-YON*) mean? Let's find out by spying out the first time this name of God is used, in Genesis 14. But first we need to put ourselves in context.

As we look at Genesis 14, we see that there is a war between four kings. These kings take Abram's nephew Lot captive. When Abram hears that Lot has been taken captive, he gathers his trained men to go and rescue him.

Let's find out what happens after Abram defeats the kings and rescues Lot. Read Genesis 14:16-20 printed out below.

> **16** He brought back all the goods, and also brought back his relative Lot with his possessions, and also the women, and the people. **17** Then after his return from the defeat of Chedorlaomer and the kings who were with him, the king of Sodom went out to meet him at the valley of Shaveh (that is, the King's Valley). **18** And Melchizedek king of Salem brought out bread and wine; now he was a priest of God Most High. **19** He blessed him and said, "Blessed be Abram of God Most High, Possessor of heaven and earth; **20** And blessed be God Most High, who has delivered your enemies into your hand." He gave him a tenth of all.

Now gather the information about God's name. Interrogate the text.

Genesis 14:18 WHAT is God's name in this verse?

God _____   _____

Genesis 14:19 WHAT do we see about God Most High? HOW is He described in this verse?_____
of _____ and _____

Look at Genesis 14:20. WHAT did God Most High do?

_____

WHAT does this Hebrew name El Elyon, God Most High, show us about God? First we see that He is the Possessor of heaven and earth. This name for God, El Elyon, shows us that God is sovereign. This means that God is the Ruler over the entire universe! There is absolutely nothing that God does not have complete and total control over! Isn't that awesome?

Now let's take a look at some other passages of Scripture that show us that God is the Ruler of all.

First let's look at Daniel 4 on page 171 to discover our Most High God. Let's put ourselves in context. Daniel 4 is about a king named Nebuchadnezzar, who was a very proud king. Nebuchadnezzar has a dream that makes him afraid. So he gives orders for the wise men and magicians to tell him what the dream means. No one can interpret the dream except for Daniel (Daniel 4:4-8).

Daniel tells Nebuchadnezzar that because the king does not recognize God as God Most High, God is going to drive him away from mankind and make him like a beast of the field. He will eat grass and be drenched with the dew of heaven for seven periods of time (seven years) (Daniel 4:24,25).

A year later Nebuchadnezzar is walking on the roof of the royal palace of Babylon and saying, "Look at all I have built by my power and might for the glory of my majesty," when a voice comes from heaven and tells King Nebuchadnezzar that his sovereignty has been removed (Daniel 4:30,31).

Let's uncover what happens next. Read Daniel 4:32-37 on your Observation Worksheet on pages 174–75.

Daniel 4:32 WHY is God going to make Nebuchadnezzar like a beast of the field for seven years? WHAT does Nebuchadnezzar need to recognize?

_____

_____

Daniel 4:33 WHAT happened?

_____

_____

Daniel 4:34 WHAT happens at the end of the seven years? WHAT does Nebuchadnezzar do?

_____

_____

Daniel 4:34,35 WHAT does Nebuchadnezzar say as He blesses and praises the Most High who lives forever? "For His dominion is an _____ dominion, and His kingdom endures from _____ to _____. All the inhabitants of the _____ are accounted as _____, but He does according to _____ _____ in the host of heaven and among the inhabitants of _____; and _____ _____ can ward off His _____ or say to Him, 'What have _____ _____?' "

Daniel 4:36 WHAT happened once Nebuchadnezzar finally recognized God as Most High God?

_____

Daniel 4:37 WHAT does Nebuchadnezzar say as he praises God? "The _____ of heaven...all His works are _____ and His ways _____, and He is able to _____ those who walk in pride."

Isn't that amazing? Did you know that God Most High humbled mighty king Nebuchadnezzar, the king of Babylon? He made him like a beast of the field. Do you know where Babylon is today? It's modern-day Iraq.

Now let's look at another passage that shows us our God Most High. Read Isaiah 14:24-27 printed out below.

> **24** The LORD of hosts has sworn saying, "Surely, just as I have intended so it has happened, and just as I have planned so it will stand, **25** to break Assyria in My land, and I will trample him on My mountains. Then his yoke will be removed from them and his burden removed from their shoulder. **26** This is the plan devised against the whole earth; and this is the hand that is stretched out against all the nations. **27** For the LORD of hosts has planned, and who can frustrate it? And as for His stretched-out hand, who can turn it back?"

Isaiah 14:24 WHAT happens to what God intends?

_____

Isaiah 14:27 WHAT do we see about the Lord of hosts?

_____

Wow! Did you know that God is the Ruler of all of the universe and that no one can stop Him? Doesn't that make you feel safe and secure, now that you know God's name is El Elyon and that He is in complete and total control? He rules over the nations, kings, rulers, and wars. We don't have to worry or be afraid, because God loves us and no one can frustrate His plans or turn back His hand! Nothing can ever happen to us without God's permission.

WHAT a discovery! Now say your memory verse one more time as you go outside to learn how to use an FAV (fast action vehicle). Aren't you glad that you have discovered just how strong God's name is this week? Call on His name, and you will be safe!

2
ACTIVATING GOD'S NAME

All right! You are on your way to becoming a secret agent for God. Look at all you have discovered so far. You know that your help, rescue, and victory is in God's name. You have discovered two of God's names: Elohim—God the Creator, and El Elyon—God Most High, the sovereign Ruler over all of the universe!

This week as we continue our secret-agent training with Uncle Matt, we need to activate God's name, El Elyon. We need to see just how awesome God Most High is so that we can rest in times of trouble, knowing that God is in absolute and total control of all our circumstances.

So let's head to the cabin. Uncle Matt is going to continue our training on maneuvering an FAV as we discover more about God Most High.

Day One

OUR VANTAGE POINT

"Watch out, Colby!" Max yelled from his go-cart as he raced past Colby. "You almost creamed Ruthi on that last bootleg turn."

"Sorry, Ruthi," Colby yelled out. "I'm getting the hang of it now!" Max, Molly, and Ruthi were laughing as they took one more spin around the field in their FAVs, practicing their evasive driving techniques to teach them how to escape the enemy by learning how to pull a bootleg turn.

"You're doing great," Uncle Matt called out as the kids drove their go-carts back to the barn and cut the engines. "You are really getting the hang of it. Bootleg turns are really difficult, but they can help you outmaneuver your enemy in a car chase. You are going to make great secret agents. Let's go wash off the dust and dirt so we can get back to our training in our Operations Manual and discover more about our Commander in Chief, Most High God."

OK, GSAs, our first assignment today is to gather more intel on God's name El Elyon. Let's read Isaiah 46:9-11 printed out below.

> **9** Remember the former things long past, for I am God, and there is no other; I am God, and there is no one like Me, **10** declaring the end from the beginning, and from ancient times things which have not been done, saying, "My purpose will be established, and I will accomplish all My good pleasure"; **11** calling a bird of prey from the east, the man of My purpose from a far country. Truly I have spoken; truly I will bring it to pass. I have planned it, surely I will do it.

Now let's make a list to see WHAT we can learn about God Most High.

Isaiah 46:9 There is no _____ like God.

Isaiah 46:10 God declares the _____ from the

_____. God's _____ will be established.

God will _____ His good

_____.

Isaiah 46:11 God calls a _____ of prey from the east

and the man of His _____from a far country.

God speaks. He will _____ it to _____.

God _____ it and He _____ do it.

Now read Daniel 2:20-23 printed out below.

> **20** Daniel said, "Let the name of God be blessed forever and ever, for wisdom and power belong to Him. **21** It is He who changes the times and the epochs; He removes kings and establishes kings; He gives wisdom to wise men and knowledge to men of understanding. **22** It is He who reveals the profound and hidden things; He knows what is in the darkness, and the light dwells with Him. **23** To You, O God of my fathers, I give thanks and praise, for You have given me wisdom and power; even now You have made known to me what we requested of You, for You have made known to us the king's matter."

WHAT does Daniel say about God?

Daniel 2:20 God's name is to be _____.

_____ and _____ belong to God.

Daniel 2:21 God _____ the _____ and the

_____.

God _____ and _____ kings.

God gives _____ to wise men and

_____ to men of understanding.

Daniel 2:22 God _____ the profound and hidden things.

God _____ what is in the _____.

The _____ dwells with Him.

Daniel 2:23 God made known to Daniel what he and the king _____.

Now read Deuteronomy 32:39 printed out below.

> *See now that I, I am He, and there is no god besides Me; it is I who put to death and give life. I have wounded and it is I who heal, and there is no one who can deliver from My hand.*

WHAT do you see about Most High God?

There is no _____ besides Him.

God puts to _____ and gives _____.

God w _ _ _ _ s and God h _ _ _ s.

There is no one who can _____ from God's hand.

Read Isaiah 45:6,7 printed out below.

> **6** That men may know from the rising to the setting of the sun that there is no one besides Me. I am the LORD, and there is no other, **7** the One forming light and creating darkness, causing

well-being and creating calamity; I am the LORD
who does all these.

WHAT do you see about God?

Isaiah 45:6 There is _____ _____ besides Him.

Isaiah 45:7 God forms _____ and creates

_____.

God causes _____ and creates

_____.

Wow! Are you surprised by what you have learned about
God? Did you notice how many times God said, "There is no
one besides Me"? God is in complete and total control. He
even decides who our rulers on earth will be.

Did you know that God is the One who wounds as well as
heals? He is the one who creates calamity—the hard and difficult situations in our lives—and well-being, which is peace.
Think about it. HOW could God be the Ruler over all if He
also was not the One who wounds, kills, and causes calamity?
You may be thinking, "But God is good! WHY would He do
these things?"

Look up and read James 1:2-4 in your Operations Manual.

James 1:4 WHAT is the perfect result of our trials?

So that we will be _____

_____

God uses the hard and difficult times in our lives to test
our faith and to make us more like Jesus or to bring us to
Jesus. He also uses wars, famines, floods, earthquakes, and
other tragedies to judge nations for their sin, as well as to
bring people to know Jesus Christ as their Savior.

Now look up and read Romans 8:28,29.

WHAT does God use for good? _____

Did you know that? God causes all things—even the bad things He allows in our lives—to work together for good.

So HOW does El Elyon use the bad things in the life of a Christian? Look at Romans 8:29. WHAT does He do with those He foreknew and predestined?

They become _____ to the image of

_____ _____.

Isn't that awesome? God uses the bad things in our lives to conform us and shape us to be more like Jesus, His Son!

All right! Now why don't you discover your new memory verse for the week by decoding Uncle Matt's rebus?

A rebus is a word puzzle that mixes pictures and words. When you combine the pictures and the letters by adding or subtracting letters, you will end up with new words.

As you decode the rebus below, write out the solution on the lines underneath the puzzle. Then practice saying the verse out loud three times in a row three times today!

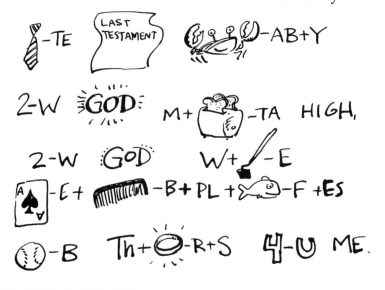

_____

_____

—Psalm 57:2

INFILTRATING THE ENEMY'S CAMP

Yesterday as we gathered more intel on God Most High, we saw just how powerful our God is. But what about our enemy? Since we have seen that God Most High means that God is sovereign and in control over everything, just WHERE does the enemy fit in?

Today let's infiltrate the enemy's camp so you can see for yourself WHO is in control—God or the enemy. Don't forget to pray and then turn to your Observation Worksheet on Job 1 on page 175. Read Job 1:6-12 and mark the following key words:

Lord (God) (draw a purple triangle and color it yellow)

Satan (draw a red pitchfork)

Now read Job 2:1-10 on pages 177–78 and mark the same key words, Lord (God) and Satan.

Good work! Now let's collect and evaluate the information on Job 1 and Job 2 by asking the 5 W's and an H questions to solve the crossword puzzle on page 47.

Job 1:8 WHO brought up Job in the conversation?

1. (Down) The _____

Job 1:10 WHY does Satan think that Job fears God?

2. (Across) Because God has made a _____ about him and his house and all that he has, on every side.

3. (Down) God has _____ the work of his hands, and his possessions have increased in the land.

WHAT do you think this hedge does for Job?

4. (Down) _ _ _ _ _ _ _ _ him. Unscramble the word in parentheses to fill in the blanks. (ectsprot)

Job 1:11 WHAT did Satan suggest that God do?
5. (Across) Put forth your _____ now and

6. (Down) _____ all that he has.

Job 1:11 WHY? WHAT did Satan think Job would do if God touched all he had?

7. (Across) "He will surely _____ You to Your face."

Job 1:12 WHAT did the Lord say to Satan?

8. (Down) "Behold, all that he has in your _____, only do not put forth your hand on him."

Job 2:3 WHAT did God point out to Satan about Job?

9. (Across) There is no one like Job on earth. He is a _____ and upright man fearing God and turning away from evil.

10. (Down) "He still holds fast his _____, although you incited Me against him to

11. (Down) _____ him without cause."

Job 2:5 WHAT was Satan's suggestion for Job this time?

12. (Across) "Touch his _____ and

13. (Down) his _____; he will curse You to Your face."

Job 2:6 WHAT was God's response?

14. (Across) "He is in your power, only spare his _____."

Now read Luke 22:31 printed out on the next page to answer the last question on your puzzle.

Simon, Simon, behold, Satan has demanded permission to sift you like wheat.

WHAT did Satan have to ask God for?

15. (Across) _____ to sift Simon like wheat

You did it! You infiltrated the camp. Now ask yourself,

WHO do we see is in control in these passages of Scripture—God or Satan? _____

HOW do you know? Think about these questions.

WHO placed the hedge around Job?

WHO gave to WHOM the power to touch Job?

WHO gave the limitation to only touching the things Job had and not Job himself?

WHO allowed Job to be touched as long as his life was spared?

Isn't that *awesome* to see that God is God Most High and in control over all our circumstances, as well as over our enemy? Satan, our enemy, only has the power that God allows him to have. He has to have God's permission to touch and test us.

Take a look at one last verse to see how Job handled the hard times that God allowed Satan to put him through. Turn to page 177 and read Job 1:21,22.

WHAT did Job know about the Lord?

"The LORD _____ and the LORD has _____
_____."

WHAT did Job say about God's name?

"_____ be the name of the LORD."

Did Job know WHO was in control? Absolutely! Did he blame God? No way! We see through all this that Job did not sin, nor did he blame God. Job knew his God, and when the hard times came, he knew that God was God Most High and that His name was still to be blessed.

Can you do that? When God allows difficult circumstances to come into your life, will you put your trust in Him in spite of the circumstances? Remember Job and be like him. Bless God's name.

Now as we leave Uncle Matt's cabin to head back to the tree house, practice saying your memory verse out loud three times in a row three times today!

CRiSiS TRAiNING—RELYiNG ON GOD'S NAME

You did a fantastic job infiltrating the enemy's camp and discovering that the enemy has to have God's permission before he can touch us! Are you amazed at all you have learned about God Most High? Today as we wrap up our mission on El Elyon, we are going to take a look at one of God's superheroes—a man named Joseph.

WHY would we call Joseph, who was an ordinary guy, a superhero? It's because Joseph knew God as El Elyon, God Most High. He trusted God in spite of all his difficult circumstances.

Let's put ourselves in context as we investigate how Joseph handled the crisis that God allowed in his life. In Genesis 37 we discover that Joseph was 17 years old and the favored son of his father, Jacob. Joseph's brothers were very jealous of him because their father loved him more than all of them. They hated him and could not speak to him on friendly terms (Genesis 37:3,4).

Because of this hate, the brothers plotted to kill Joseph. They stripped him of his special varicolored tunic, a gift from their father, and threw him into a pit. Judah (one of the brothers) later convinces the other brothers to sell Joseph instead of killing him, and Joseph is sold as a slave in Egypt to Potiphar.

So we see that Joseph has gone from being popular with Papa, to being thrown in a pit, to being sold as a slave to Potiphar. Is life easy for this man who loves God? No way! WHAT happens next? While Joseph is Potiphar's slave, he is accused of something he didn't do and is thrown into prison for two very long years!

Can you believe it? HOW would you feel if you were kidnapped by your own brothers, sold as a slave, and then put in jail for two long years for something you didn't even do?

Most people would be angry or bitter at God, but what did Joseph do? Joseph honored God. He never grew angry or bitter. He put his faith in God Most High. Even when he didn't understand, he knew that God had a purpose for it all.

HOW do we know that Joseph honored God and knew God was in control of all his circumstances? Let's grab our Operations Manuals, our Bibles, and discover it for ourselves. After Joseph has been in prison for two years, he is brought out to help Pharaoh, who has had two dreams that no one can interpret. Look up and read Genesis 40:8.

To WHOM did Joseph say the interpretations belonged?

_____

Read Genesis 41:25-28.

Genesis 41:25-28 To WHOM does Joseph point Pharaoh?

_____

Even though Joseph has been mistreated by his brothers, sold as a slave in Egypt, falsely accused, and thrown in prison, to WHOM does he tell Pharaoh the interpretations belong? To WHOM does Joseph point Pharaoh to as being in control? God! Joseph knows God is God Most High, El Elyon.

Read Genesis 45:4-8.

Genesis 45:5 WHAT does Joseph say to his brothers when he reveals himself to them? _____

_____

Genesis 45:7,8 WHO sent Joseph to Egypt?

_____

We see that Joseph knows that God is God Most High, in control of all his circumstances. He recognizes that even though his brothers sold him, God was the One in charge.

Genesis 45:7 WHY did God send Joseph to Egypt?

_____

Now let's read Genesis 50:18-21.

Genesis 50:19,20 WHAT were the brothers' intentions?

_____

Genesis 50:20 WHAT were God's intentions?

_____

Genesis 50:21 HOW did Joseph treat the brothers who had mistreated him?

_____

You have just seen for yourself that Joseph knew God as the sovereign Ruler of the universe. He knew that God was the Giver of the interpretations of the dreams, and he knew that God was the One who sent him to Egypt. He knew that even though his brothers meant what happened to him for evil, God meant it for good to provide a great deliverance and to keep them alive during a famine. Joseph was able to bow his knee and surrender his will for God's, even in the hard and difficult times in his life. What a superhero!

Now read 1 Thessalonians 5:18 printed out below.

> *In everything give thanks; for this is God's will for you in Christ Jesus.*

WHAT is God's will for you?

_____

Will you do that? Will you give thanks to God, even in the hard times, instead of complaining? Remember what we just saw in Joseph's life, how God took the bad and the ugly and used it to save an entire nation. God also has a plan for you! Don't forget what you learned in Romans 8:28:

> *And we know that God causes all things to work together for good to those who love God, to those who are called according to His purpose.*

Because we know WHO God is, that He is El Elyon, Most High God, Ruler over all the universe, we can lean on this promise in Romans that God will use the bad things in our lives for good. We can bow our knees in surrender and give thanks to God in all things!

FOR YOUR EYES ONLY

"Hey, guys," Uncle Matt called out as the kids headed to the front door of the cabin. "Are you ready for your next mission of discovering another one of God's aliases?"

"We sure are!" Max, Molly, Colby, and Ruthi all agreed.

"All right, then here we go. Inside this envelope is a riddle. Once you solve it, it will help you figure out where the next encoded secret message is that contains God's name." Max opened the envelope and started reading the riddle out loud to Molly, Ruthi, Colby, and Sam.

"I exist naturally in all three states of matter. I can be a liquid, a gas, or a solid. When I am a liquid, I take on the shape of my container. When I get hot I become all steamed up. When I get very, very cold, I expand and become a solid. WHAT am I?"

"Oh, I know," an excited Colby yelled out. "It's water!"

"That's right!" Ruthi added. "Water is a liquid, and when it gets hot and turns into steam, it's a gas. When it's frozen it expands and becomes a solid!"

"Way to go, guys!" replied Uncle Matt. "You are so smart! Now all you have to do is discover where the next secret message is hidden."

Max started thinking out loud. "OK, since Uncle Matt's riddle gives us all three states of water, let's check out each one. Molly, why don't you and Ruthi check out the places where we would find water as a liquid. Colby, you take water as a gas. Why don't you check out the teakettle in the kitchen and around the stove area? I'll take water as a solid. I'll check out Uncle Matt's freezer. Come on, guys. Let's go."

As Max opened the freezer door, he noticed that not only did Uncle Matt have an automatic ice maker, but he also had a plastic tray of ice cubes. "Hey, Colby, come over here and take a look. Why would Uncle Matt need an ice tray if he has an automatic ice maker?"

"Good question, Max. Let's check it out."

Molly and Ruthi arrived in the kitchen just as Max called out, "Look, there's something frozen in one of the ice cubes. Let's thaw it out."

"Hey, it's a key," Ruthi exclaimed as the ice melted. "Now all we have to do is find what it unlocks."

"I think I know, Ruthi," Max answered. "Yesterday Uncle Matt put a lockbox on the bookshelf while he was talking to us. Let's go check it out." Max pulled the locked box off the shelf and tried the key in the lock. It clicked open to reveal an envelope inside labeled "GSA Team."

"We found it, Uncle Matt," Max called out as he held up the envelope for Uncle Matt to inspect.

"Great work, Max!" Uncle Matt replied. "I deliberately put that box away in front of you yesterday to see if you would remember and put two and two together. You are becoming quite a spy! Now open the envelope up and discover the next Hebrew name for God."

OK, GSAs, now it's your turn to get to work. Decode the secret message below by coloring the spaces that have a dot in them red and writing the code word on the line underneath the puzzle.

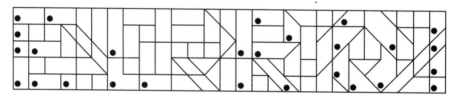

_____

Mission complete! Now WHAT does this name of God mean? Let's find out. Turn to your Observation Worksheet on Genesis 16 on page 178 and let's spy out the meaning of God's name El Roi (pronounced *el roy*). Read Genesis 16 and mark the following key words:

God (draw a purple triangle and color it yellow)

Abram (color it blue)

Hagar (color it orange)

Sarai (color it pink)

Now let's discover the mystery of God's name El Roi.

Genesis 16:3 WHOM did Sarai give to Abram to become his wife?

_____

Genesis 16:4,5 WHAT happened after Hagar conceived Abram's child? She d ___ ___ ___ ___ ___ ___ d Sarai. This word *despised* means "to make light of, to be lessened or insignificant, to put down." This could mean that once Hagar was pregnant, she thought less of Sarai and could have made fun of her or rubbed it in that she was pregnant and Sarai was not.

Genesis 16:6 HOW did Sarai treat Hagar?

_____

WHAT does Hagar do?

_____

Genesis 16:7 WHO finds Hagar? _____

Genesis 16:9 WHAT does the angel of the Lord tell her to do?

"_____ to your _____, and

_____ yourself to her _____."

Genesis 16:10 WHAT does the angel of the Lord tell her He will do?

_____

Genesis 16:11,12 WHAT does the angel of the Lord tell her about the child she is pregnant with?

"You will bear a _____."

"You shall call his name _____."

"He will be a _____ _____ of a man."

"His _____ will be against _____,

and everyone's _____ will be against him."

"He will live to the _____ of all his

_____."

Genesis 16:13 WHAT does Hagar call the name of the Lord?

"You are a _____ who _____."

The mystery is solved. Genesis 16:13 shows us the meaning of this Hebrew name for God, El Roi. Isn't that awesome? God sees. God saw what happened to Hagar. He knew about her affliction, her pain, and her distress. God saw her run away, and He sent the angel of the Lord to let her know that He cared.

God loves us. He sees everything that happens to us. We cannot run away and hide from Him. God also sent Hagar back home to deal with the painful situation with Sarai. God does not want us to run away from our problems. He wants us to know that He sees what happens to us, and He will use those bad things for good. Look at what God told Hagar would happen. She would have a son!

Now look up and read Psalm 139:7-12 on page 166 of your Observation Worksheets.

Can you flee from God's presence, or is God with you wherever you are?

_____

Now read Proverbs 5:21 printed out below.

For the ways of a man are before the eyes of the LORD, and He watches all his paths.

WHAT do we find out about the Lord?

_____

WHAT does the Lord watch?

_____

Doesn't that comfort you, knowing that God sees everything that happens to you?

Read Psalm 9:10 printed out below.

> *And those who know Your name will put their trust in You, for You, O LORD, have not forsaken those who seek You.*

Remember what you learned today the next time someone at school hurts your feelings, or talks about you behind your back, or when you think you have messed up and just want to die. Don't run away or get even. Don't give up. Instead run straight to God, your El Roi. He sees. He cares. He will heal your hurt. He will not forsake, abandon, or turn His back on you! He uses even the hard, difficult, and bad things for good!

GOING OUT IN THE OPEN—GOD IS OUR STRENGTH

"Hey, guys. Guess what I found under my pillow this morning?" Molly asked Max, Colby, and Ruthi as she rode up on her bike.

"What?" Max asked.

"A secret message. Isn't that cool?"

"Really?" Max asked in astonishment. "Right under your pillow? Uncle Matt sure is a great secret agent. Let's head over to the lake right now and find out how to decode it."

"All right! Let's go!" yelled Colby, Ruthi, and Molly, while Sam started howling to make sure he wouldn't miss out on being part of the action.

"Hey, Uncle Matt," Max called out, "Molly found your secret message."

"Way to go, Molly! Why don't we pray together, and then you can pull out your codebooks and decode the message to discover another one of God's names."

OK, GSAs, now that we have prayed, let's get to work. Break the number code in Molly's secret message by using the Number Cipher Secret Code in your codebook. Find the letter of the alphabet that matches the number in the code and write the correct letters under the encoded message.

Molly's secret message:

10-24   38-16-2-8-8-2-18

_____   _____

NUMBER CIPHER SECRET CODE

A	B	C	D	E	F	G	H	I	J	K	L	M
2	4	6	8	10	12	14	16	18	20	22	24	26

N	O	P	Q	R	S	T	U	V	W	X	Y	Z
28	30	32	34	36	38	40	42	44	46	48	50	52

You did it! Now read Genesis 17:1-6 printed out below.

1 Now when Abram was ninety-nine years old, the LORD appeared to Abram and said to him, "I am God Almighty; walk before Me, and be blameless. **2** I will establish My covenant between Me and you, and I will multiply you exceedingly." **3** Abram fell on his face, and God talked with him, saying, **4** "As for Me, behold, My covenant is with you, and you will be the father of a multitude of nations. **5** No longer shall your name be called Abram, but your name shall be Abraham; for I will make you the father of a multitude of nations. **6** I will make you exceedingly fruitful, and I will make nations of you, and kings will come forth from you."

All right, GSAs! Gather the intel and discover the meaning of God's Hebrew name El Shaddai.

Genesis 17:1 HOW old is Abram?

_____ years old

Abram was 75 years old in Genesis 12:4 when God promised that He would make him a great nation, and now we see he is 99 years old.

HOW long has it been since God's promise?

_____ years

Abram has been waiting all these years for God to give him and Sarai a child, and now he is 99 years old—way past the age of having children.

Look at Genesis 17:1 as God appears to Abram. WHO does God tell Abram He is? "I am _____

_____."

You have just discovered the meaning of God's name El Shaddai. *El Shaddai* (pronounced *el sha-DIE*) is translated as "God Almighty." This name of God means just what it says. God is the almighty One, the powerful or mighty One. God is all-sufficient. He is all that we need.

Genesis 17:3 WHAT does Abram do when he meets God as El Shaddai?

_____

Genesis 17:4 WHAT is God going to make Abram the father of?

_____

Did you notice that Abram falls on his face when he encounters God as El Shaddai? Abram is 99 years old, without any children, yet God is promising he will be the father of a multitude of nations. HOW can that happen? There is only one way: through El Shaddai. God is all-sufficient. He is God Almighty. He can do anything!

Genesis 17:5 WHAT does God do in this verse?

He changes Abram's name to _____.

God adds something to Abram's name. He adds the letter *He,* ה—the chief letter of His own name Jehovah—the sound that can only be uttered by an outbreathing. God breathes into Abram part of Himself. God has promised that kings and nations would come from Abram. Now He changes Abram's name, which means "exalted" or "high father," to Abraham, which means "father of a multitude," to reflect that promise.

When Abram was weak, we see that God is strong. God was able to give Abram a child and make him the father of a multitude, even though Abram was past the age to father a child. God is our El Shaddai, our all-sufficient One. He is our rock and our refuge in times of trouble. When we are weak, He is strong. He is Almighty God. He has all the power you will ever need.

Now read 2 Corinthians 12:9,10 printed out below.

9 And He has said to me, "My grace is sufficient for you, for power is perfected in weakness." Most gladly, therefore, I will rather boast about my weaknesses, so that the power of Christ may dwell in me. **10** Therefore I am well content with weaknesses, with insults, with distresses, with persecutions, with difficulties, for Christ's sake; for when I am weak, then I am strong."

2 Corinthians 12:9 WHAT is sufficient for you?

_____

HOW is power perfected?

_____

WHEN does Christ's power dwell in us?

_____

Isn't that *awesome?* When we are weak, we don't have to worry because God is strong! Remember these verses the next time you feel weak and powerless. Remember that God is El Shaddai. He has all the power you will ever need!

Fantastic! Now before you head out to do a little physical training, why don't you say your memory verse to a grown-up to help you remember just WHO will accomplish all things for you when you cry out to Him!

3

RECON AND RESCUE—GOD IS LORD

How do you like learning about being a spy so far? Pretty cool, isn't it? This week as we head out on a mission of recon and rescue, we are going to discover a very important name for God. Are you ready? Great! Then let's head to the park to meet Max, Molly, Ruthi, Colby, and Sam to get started on our next secret mission.

UNCOVERING GOD'S IDENTITY

"Hey, guys, we're right over here behind these bushes," Max called out as you approached the bushes behind the swing sets. "Grab your binoculars and help us do our recon by scouting out the territory. Uncle Matt has sent us back to the park to discover our next contact.

"This is the info that we have: 'I am a colonel incognito in red and white stripes. Have Colby approach the contact wearing his sunglasses to ask if the colonel is freshly popped.' "

"A colonel," Molly repeated as she looked through her binoculars. "Do you see anyone dressed like a colonel with red and white stripes?"

"No," Ruthi replied as she scanned the park through her binoculars. "I sure don't see anyone in a military uniform. Hey, wait a minute." Ruthi paused and giggled and lowered her binoculars as she turned to Molly and Max. "Your Uncle Matt is pretty sneaky."

"Why do you say that, Ruthi?" Max asked. "Do you see something?"

"I think so," Ruthi smiled. "Look through your binoculars. OK, now what do you see over there by the balloon man?"

Colby answered, "You mean the girl selling popcorn?"

"Um-hum." Ruthi continued to smile. "What is popcorn before it's popped?"

Max started grinning. "Kernels," he answered. "I get it. Uncle Matt is sneaky. Our colonel is really a kernel. Look at the popcorn boxes: red and white stripes. I bet this is it, GSAs. Great work, Ruthi. Now it's your turn, Colby. Go retrieve our secret message. Ask if the 'colonel' is freshly popped."

"All right, here I go. Come on, Sam. You can be my back-up. Let's go out in the open and retrieve the next secret code."

In a few minutes Colby was back with a box of popcorn and a very excited and yapping Sam. "Where do you think the message is, Max?"

"I don't know. Last time it was in the balloon. Let's eat the popcorn to see if it's at the bottom of the box."

As Colby threw Sam the last piece of popcorn, he announced, "It's empty. What do we do now?"

WHERE do you think the secret message is, GSAs? Do you have a clue? Why don't you head to the lake with Max, Molly, Ruthi, Colby, and Sam to check in with Uncle Matt?

"Hey, Uncle Matt," Molly called out, "we discovered the 'colonel.' But all we got was a box of freshly popped popcorn. Where's the secret message?"

Uncle Matt smiled as he looked at Colby holding the empty box. "Did you check out the box?"

"We sure did," Colby answered as he took a closer look at the box. "Hey, this box has POPCORN written on one side, but what's this word on the other side? 'PRKJPE?' "

"I believe that's your secret message," Uncle Matt replied. "Do any of you have an idea what kind of secret code was used to encode this message?"

"Hmmmm," Molly thought out loud. "Since the box has the word *popcorn* on one side and the secret message on the other, could this be a code that is broken by using a key word?"

"That's it, Molly. You have cracked the code. Since *popcorn* is our key word, the first thing we do is write out our key word like this: POPCORN.

"Now we have to get rid of all the repeated letters. This is what we are left with: POCRN. We start our secret alphabet off with the letters that are left from our key word. Then after the letter *N* we start writing out the regular alphabet, skipping the letters that we have already used in our key word.

"After we finish, we line the real or clear alphabet up under our encoded one. Check out the Key Word Secret Code in your top secret notebook below. To decode the secret message on the box of popcorn, find the letter in the real or clear alphabet under the encoded one and write out the real letters on the line under your secret message."

KEY WORD SECRET CODE

P O C R N A B D E F G H I J K L M Q S T U V W X Y Z

A B C D E F G H I J K L M N O P Q R S T U V W X Y Z

PRKJPE

All right! You just cracked another secret code! So what does this Hebrew name *Adonai* (pronounced *a-doh-NIE*) mean? Let's find out.

Read Genesis 15:1-6 printed out below to see the first time this name for God is used. Then ask the 5 W's and an H to uncover the meaning of God's name Adonai.

> **1** After these things the word of the LORD came to Abram in a vision, saying, "Do not fear, Abram, I am a shield to you; your reward shall be very great." **2** Abram said, "O Lord GOD, what will You give me, since I am childless, and the heir of my house is Eliezer of Damascus?" **3** And Abram said, "Since You have given no offspring to me, one born in my house is my heir." **4** Then behold, the word of the LORD came to him, saying, "This man will not be your heir; but one who will come forth from your own body, he shall be your heir." **5** And He took him outside and said, "Now look toward the heavens, and count the stars, if you are able to count them." And He said to him, "So shall your descendants be." **6** Then he believed in the LORD; and He reckoned it to him as righteousness.

> Genesis 15:2 HOW does Abram address God in this verse?

> "O _____ GOD"

That's it, GSAs. That's the meaning of God's name Adonai. This name of God means "Lord." God is our Lord, Master, and Owner. Did you know that? WHAT does it mean for us to know God as our Lord? Let's find out. First let's put ourselves in context.

In Genesis 12 God had told Abram that He is going to make him a great nation. Yet at this point Abram still doesn't have any children, so Abram asks God, his Lord and Master, what God is going to give him since he is childless. He asks

God if it will be through Eliezer, his heir, that he will be made a great nation. Let's see what God says.

Genesis 15:4 WHO did God say would be Abram's heir?

_____

Genesis 15:5 WHAT did God tell Abram about his descendants?

_____

Genesis 15:6 WHAT does Abram do?

_____

WHAT did God do?

He _____ it to him as _____.

Do you know what it means for it to be reckoned to him as righteousness? A righteous man is a person who has been made right with God. HOW was Abram made right with God? He believed God. WHAT did he believe? Let's take a look at a cross-reference. Look up and read Galatians 3:6-8.

Galatians 3:8 WHAT did God preach to Abraham?

_____

God preached the gospel—the good news of Jesus coming to die on a cross to save Abraham from his sins. Abraham believed God, and God saved him. That's what it means to be made righteous. A person is made righteous when he realizes he is a sinner and confesses his sins. He has asked Jesus to be his Savior and now has a right relationship with God. He wants to do what God says is right in His Word.

Abram first recognizes God as his Lord and Master, the Owner of his life, in Genesis 15:2. Later, in Genesis 15:6, we see Abram believing God. We see Abram's salvation.

Wow! So WHAT does it mean for God to be Lord in your life? Letting God be the Lord and Master of your life means that you have to surrender your will to God's. It is to bow the knee to Adonai. You have to let God take over and rule your life. You have to obey God by doing the things He tells you to do in His Word.

So WHAT is God's will for your life? Read John 6:40 printed out below.

> *For this is the will of My Father, that everyone who beholds the Son and believes in Him will have eternal life, and I Myself will raise him up on the last day.*

John 6:40 WHAT is God's will?

_____

WHAT does it mean to believe in the Son? Let's find out. But first, WHO is God's Son? _____

Look up and read John 10:30 on page 191 of your Observation Worksheets. This is Jesus speaking.

WHAT does Jesus say in John 10:30?

_____

Jesus is making it very clear that He and God are both God. To believe in Jesus is to believe that Jesus is not only God's Son, but that Jesus is also God! So if we bow the knee and surrender to God as Adonai, we also have to acknowledge Jesus as Adonai and surrender our lives to Him because Jesus is God. To believe in Jesus is to believe that Jesus is God. Do you believe that?

WHAT else do we have to believe to be saved? Look up and read Romans 10:9,10 in your Operations Manual.

> Romans 10:9 WHAT do you have to confess with your mouth?

_____

WHAT do you have to believe in your heart so that you will be saved?

_____

Now look up and read Matthew 1:21. WHAT will Jesus save His people from? _____

Not only do you have to believe that Jesus is God and that He died and was raised again, but you also have to know that you are a sinner. The reason Jesus left heaven to come to earth was to die on the cross to pay the price for your sins. Do you realize you are a sinner?

WHAT is sin? Read James 4:17 printed out below.

> *Therefore, to one who knows the right thing to do and does not do it, to him it is sin.*

WHAT is sin?

_____

Read Romans 3:23 printed out below.

> *For all have sinned and fall short of the glory of God.*

WHO has sinned? _____

That means everyone, including you and me!

WHAT causes us to sin? Look up and read Isaiah 53:6 to find out where sin comes from. WHAT is the root of sin? HOW are we like sheep?

All of us like sheep have _____ _____.

Each of us has _____ to _____ _____

_____.

That's the root of sin: wanting our own way instead of obeying God and doing things His way.

Now look up and read Luke 15:7.
WHAT is there more joy in heaven over?

_____

Do you know what it means to repent of your sins? It
means to change your mind about your sins, to realize that sin
is wrong and decide to turn away from your sins. It is to want
to do things God's way.

Before you can ever let God be your Adonai, the Lord and
Master of your life, you have to be saved. We have just seen
what it means to be saved.

First you have to know WHO Jesus is—that He is our
Savior, that He is God's Son, that He is God, and that He lived
a perfect life without sin and died on a cross to pay for our
sins. Then He was buried, and God raised Him from the dead.
Then you have to know that you are a sinner and be willing to
confess those sins to God and turn away from them. You have
to be willing to turn your entire life over to God—Adonai.

Have you accepted Jesus Christ as your Savior? Have you
received God's free gift of salvation (Ephesians 2:8,9) and
turned your life over to God? If so, then you are ready to continue your mission of discovering what it means for God to be
your Lord.

If you haven't, then you can receive this gift of salvation
right now. All you have to do is come to God and ask. You
need to admit that you are a sinner (Romans 3:23—"For all
have sinned and fall short of the glory of God"). Tell God that
you are sorry for your sins and want to be a follower of Jesus
Christ.

You can pray a prayer like this:

> _Thank You, God, for loving me and sending Your Son
> Jesus Christ to die for my sins. I am sorry for the things
> I have done wrong. I am repenting, changing my mind
> about my sins. Sin is wrong. I don't want to do things
> my way anymore. I want to receive Jesus Christ as my
> Savior, and now I turn my entire life over to You. Amen._

If you prayed this prayer, then you have been reckoned as righteous, just like Abram. You are a part of God's family! You are God's child, and Jesus and the Holy Spirit will come to live in you (John 14:23). Why don't you go back to the prayer on page 70 and write today's date next to the Amen to remind you of the day that God saved you from your sins?

Now that you have become a part of God's family, you will want to share this great news by telling other people (confessing with your mouth) that you have believed in Jesus Christ and are now a child of God.

Way to go! Now that we have been rescued from our sins, let's go do a little physical training. Tomorrow we will discover more about letting God be our Adonai.

ACTIVATING GOD'S NAME

Guess what? Since we are doing so well with our physical training, Uncle Matt has decided to start our martial arts training today. But first we need to finish gathering the intel on what it means for God to be Adonai—Lord, Master, and Owner of our lives.

Let's get started. Why don't you pray, and then we will be good to go. Pull out those Operations Manuals, and let's look up and read Luke 6:46.

WHAT is Jesus asking in this verse?

_____

Can you call Jesus Lord of your life if you do not obey Him? ____

Look up and read Malachi 1:6.

WHAT is the Lord of hosts asking when He says, "If I am a master, WHERE is My _____?"

HOW can God be your Master if you do not respect and honor Him?

If God is to be the Master and Owner of our lives, then we have to submit to whatever He asks us to do. We have to surrender our desires for God's. We need to say, "God, I want Your will for my life instead of my will." Just as a servant's responsibility is to obey and serve his master, if God is the Lord of our life, then we will obey and serve God. And just like a master provides for the needs of his servant, God will provide for our needs.

Read Matthew 7:21-27 printed out below. This is Jesus speaking.

21 Not everyone who says to Me, "Lord, Lord," will enter the kingdom of heaven, but he who does the will of My Father who is in heaven will enter. 22 Many will say to Me on that day, "Lord, Lord, did we not prophesy in Your name, and in Your name cast out demons, and in Your name perform many miracles?" 23 And then I will declare to them, "I never knew you; depart from Me, you who practice lawlessness." 24 Therefore everyone who hears these words of Mine and acts on them, may be compared to a wise man who built his house on the rock. 25 And the rain fell, and the floods came, and the winds blew and slammed against that house; and [yet] it did not fall, for it had been founded on the rock. 26 Everyone who hears these words of Mine and does not act on them, will be like a foolish man who built his house on the sand. 27 The rain fell, and the floods came, and the winds blew and slammed against that house; and it fell—and great was its fall.

Now gather the intel. Ask the 5 W's and an H questions. Matthew 7:21 Will everyone who calls Jesus "Lord" enter the kingdom of heaven? _____

WHO will enter the kingdom of heaven?

_____

Can you be saved if you just call Jesus "Lord" but do not surrender and let Jesus truly be the Master and Owner of your life? _____

Matthew 7:22,23 WHAT will happen to those who did good things but not the Father's will?

_____

Matthew 7:24,25 WHO are you like if you hear God's words and act on them?

_____

Matthew 7:26,27 WHO are you like if you hear God's words but don't act on them?

_____

Are you willing to let Jesus be your Master, your God? Are you willing to bow the knee and say, "I only want what You want, Lord"? Are you willing to obey God's Word? _____

WHO are you like: the wise man or the foolish man?

_____

Now let's look up and read one more verse: Mark 8:34.

WHAT do you have to do if you wish to come after Jesus? _____ myself, take up my _____, and _____ Jesus.

Are you willing to deny yourself and put Jesus first in your life? That's what it takes for Him to truly be your Adonai.

If you are willing for God and Jesus to truly be your Adonai, write out a commitment to God on the lines below. Just tell Him that you are willing to surrender your desires for His, and you want to deny yourself and let Him be the Lord of your life.

_____

_____

_____

_____

Awesome intel! Now let's discover this week's memory verse by using our Key Word Secret Code for *popcorn* that we discovered yesterday.

KEY WORD SECRET CODE

P O C R N A B D E F G H I J K L M Q S T U V W X Y Z
A B C D E F G H I J K L M N O P Q R S T U V W X Y Z

Take a look at your encoded memory verse below. Now use the Key Word Secret Code to decode this verse.

E   SPER   TK   TDN   HKQR,   "YKU   PQN   IY

___ _____ ___ ___ _____ _____ ___ __

HKQR;   E   DPVN   JK   BKKR   ONSERNS   YKU."

_____ __ ____ ___ ____ _____ ____

LSPHI 16:2

_____

Great decoding! As you head outside to meet your martial arts instructor, Mr. Tim, practice saying this verse out loud three times in a row to remind yourself just WHO God is to you!

juLieT-ecHO-HOTeL-OscAR-VicTOR-ALpHA-HOTeL

"You guys did great learning martial arts," Uncle Matt told Max, Molly, Ruthi, and Colby as he came to pass out lemonade. "I especially loved Sam's moves."

"What moves?" Max laughed. "You mean when Sam grabbed onto Mr. Tim's pants and growled as Mr. Tim was going to flip me?"

"Yes," Uncle Matt laughed. "That's the one." Everyone laughed as Sam sat there panting, proud to have defended his master. "Well, are you guys ready for your next training assignment?"

"We sure are!"

"Then let's go. As you head onto the obstacle course today, I want you to keep your eyes open. The secret message is hidden somewhere on the course. Whoever finds it first needs to head back here without letting the others know he has discovered the message. Ring the bell to signal that the mission has been accomplished."

"That sounds like fun!" Colby yelled. "Let's go!"

Uncle Matt smiled as he watched them out on the course. He saw Ruthi look around and grab onto the zip line to head toward home base. As Ruthi jumped off the zip line and started running, Max turned and sounded the alarm.

Uncle Matt laughed as Ruthi rang the bell and sank onto the back porch. "You almost made it back unnoticed, but here they come now!"

This is what the secret message said:

Juliet-Echo-Hotel-Oscar-Victor-Alpha-Hotel

OK, GSAs, do you know how to figure out this name of God? Did you know that the Army has a chart that uses different words to stand for the letters of the alphabet? They use these words when they communicate by radio so they can understand exactly what is being communicated. This is because some letters of the alphabet sound the same, and some people have different accents, and sometimes the quality of their radio communication is not clear.

Secret agents also use this code when they are out in the field. So get some practice in. Below is the Army chart. Use it to spell out God's name by writing the letter that stands for each word of the secret message in the blanks below.

Juliet-Echo-Hotel-Oscar-Victor-Alpha-Hotel

___ ___ ___ ___ ___ ___ ___

Mission complete! Now let's discover what this name of God means. *Jehovah* is the most frequent used name for God in the Old Testament. The Hebrew letters are YHWH. Are you ready for a big word? These four letters are frequently called "Tetragrammaton." Did you notice there are four consonants and no vowels? Some people add the vowels "e," "o," and "a" and change the "Y" to a "J" and the "w" to a "v" to get *Jehovah*, pronounced je-HOE-vah. Others add only the vowels "a" and "e" to get *Yahweh* (YAH-way), linking the name to the Hebrew verb *hâyâh*, meaning "to be, to exist."

Jehovah, or Yahweh, implies a Being who is absolutely self-existent. That means God always was, is, and always will be. He doesn't need anything outside of Himself. Nobody made God! Rather, He is the Creator of all. The first time this name of God (Jehovah) is used in the Bible is in Genesis 2:4.

> *This is the account of the heavens and the earth when they were created, in the day that the* LORD *God made earth and heaven.*

The name for God in this verse is Elohim, God the Creator, but look at the name that comes before God: LORD. This is the name for Jehovah (YHWH). Anytime you see the name LORD in all capital letters (or capital and small capital letters) in the Bible, it is the name Jehovah, the self-existent One.

But WHAT if we see *Lord* written with a capital L and then the rest of the letters are lowercase? Do you remember the name of God we learned that means God is our Lord and Master? WHAT is it? Write it out here: _____

The first time we see the name Jehovah, it is with the name Elohim, Creator. That shows us that the self-existent God who has always been is the One who brought everything into being.

Jehovah is the most holy, glorious name of God. It was a name that made the Jews afraid and filled them with awe. It was so sacred that they would not even pronounce it. Did you know that every time they wrote the name Jehovah they would stop, take off their clothes, take a complete bath, put on clean clothes, and then use a pen that had never been used before to write the name Jehovah? That's how holy and sacred this name is for God! Even though this name is used in Genesis, it isn't until Exodus that God reveals just what this name means.

Let's discover more about this holy name of God. Turn to your Observation Worksheet on Exodus 3 on page 180. Read Exodus 3:1-15 and mark LORD and God by drawing a purple triangle and coloring it yellow.

Now gather the intel.

Exodus 3:2 HOW does the angel of the LORD appear to Moses?

_____

Exodus 3:5 WHAT does God tell Moses to do?

_____

WHY? _____

Exodus 3:6 WHY did Moses hide his face?

_____

Exodus 3:7 WHAT has God seen?

_____

Exodus 3:8 WHAT has God come down to do?

_____

Exodus 3:14 WHAT does God say to Moses?

_____

WHAT was the name God told Moses to use to tell the sons of Israel who had sent him to them?

_____

Exodus 3:15 WHAT did God say His name was?

_____

Is this name in all capitals? _____

WHAT does God say about this name in verse 15?

_____

This is the name for Jehovah. He is the eternal I AM, the Alpha (the beginning) and Omega (the end), who is the same yesterday, today, and forever. All of life is in Him. He has never failed. He is the self-existent, covenant-keeping God. He keeps His promises. He does what He says He will do. He never changes. He is the I AM.

Read Hebrews 13:5,6 printed out below.

> **5**...for He Himself has said, "I will never desert you, nor will I ever forsake you," **6** so that we confidently say, "The LORD is my helper, I will not be afraid. What will man do to me?"

WHAT do we see about the LORD, the eternal I AM?

"I will _____ _____ you, nor will I ever _____ you."

"The LORD is my _____, I will not be _____."

Now read Exodus 34:6,7 printed out below.

> **6** Then the LORD passed by in front of him and proclaimed, "The LORD, the LORD God, compassionate and gracious, slow to anger, and abounding in lovingkindness and truth; **7** who keeps lovingkindness for thousands, who forgives iniquity, transgression and sin; yet He will by no means leave the guilty unpunished, visiting the iniquity of fathers on the children and on the grandchildren to the third and fourth generations."

WHAT do you see about the character of God? Write down the adjectives that describe the LORD God from these two verses on the lines below.

_____

_____

Just look at all you see about the LORD God! Jehovah is compassionate and gracious, slow to anger, and abounding in lovingkindness and truth. He forgives iniquity, transgression, and sin. He does not leave the guilty unpunished. He is an awesome God!

Jehovah is all that you will ever need! When you feel lonely, you need to remember God's name is Jehovah. He will never leave you nor forsake you. He is your Helper. You do not have to be afraid. Just run to Him and trust in His name!

OPERATION OBSERVATION—WHAT DO YOU SEE?

"Hey, guys. How did Operation Observation go on your bike ride from the tree house through the park to the cabin?" Uncle Matt asked as they headed inside the cabin.

"Great! Check out the sketches in my notebook," Molly answered.

"All right. Let's take a look." Uncle Matt scanned through each one of their sketches in their notebooks. "Great observations. You did your homework. Now take a closer look at the order of your sketches to see if you can discover how to uncover God's name."

"I think I get it, Uncle Matt," Max replied. "Does God's code name come from the first letter of the alphabet from each of these sketches?"

"It sure does," Uncle Matt replied. "OK, GSAs, break the code by looking at the pictures on the next page. WHAT letter of the alphabet does each object start with? Use the first letter from each one of these pictures to spell out God's name."

---------   ---------   ---------   ---------   ---------   ---------   ---------

---------   ---------   ---------   ---------   ---------

Way to go! WHAT does this name, *Jehovah-jireh* (pronounced *je-HOE-vah JIE-rah*) mean? Let's find out. Don't forget to pray, and then turn to page 182. Read Genesis 22 and mark the following key words and key phrase:

The LORD Will Provide (underline it in blue)

love (draw a red heart)

obey (circle it in orange and color it yellow)

worship (circle it in purple and color it blue)

Now uncover the meaning. Ask the 5 W's and an H.

Genesis 22:2 WHAT was Isaac to Abraham, and HOW did Abraham feel about Isaac?

Isaac was Abraham's only _____ whom he

_____.

God uses the word *love* here for the first time in the Bible to show a father offering up his only son.

Does this remind you of another Father who offered up His only Son?

WHO was God's only begotten Son?

_____

Genesis 22:1,2 WHY was Abraham going to offer up his son?

Because _____ told him to take his son and offer him as a burnt offering

Genesis 22:2 WHAT land would he make the sacrifice in?

The land of _____

Genesis 22:2 WHERE in this land would the sacrifice be made?

On one of the _____ of which God would tell him

WHAT kind of sacrifice was it?

A _____ _____.

Genesis 22:5 WHAT does Abraham call this sacrifice?

WHAT does he tell his young men that he and Isaac will do?

"We will _____ and return to you."

Genesis 22:6 WHAT did Abraham lay on Isaac?

The _____ of the burnt offering

Look up and read John 19:17. WHAT did Jesus carry?

His own _____

Genesis 22:8 WHAT does Abraham tell Isaac that God will do?

"God will _____ for Himself the _____ for the burnt offering."

WHY did God tell Abraham to offer up Isaac?

Genesis 22:1 God _____ Abraham.

Genesis 22:12 To see if Abraham f _____ d God and

to see if Abraham would withhold his _____ son

from God

Genesis 22:13 WHAT did Abraham offer to God in

Isaac's place?

A _____

Genesis 22:14 WHAT did Abraham name that place?

The _____ Will _____

WHY? Because "in the _____ of the LORD it will

be _____."

Genesis 22:18 WHY would all the nations of the earth be

blessed?

Because Abraham _____ God's voice.

Now go back and find all the answers from our questions and circle them in the word search below. If a word is used more than once, you only need to find and circle it one time.

M	X	E	P	R	O	V	I	D	E	G	Y
O	F	F	E	R	I	N	G	L	J	O	A
U	T	Y	L	N	O	B	E	Y	E	D	O
N	T	N	R	U	B	V	P	Y	S	L	R
T	H	E	U	H	R	R	I	I	U	O	L
A	K	O	S	O	A	Q	H	D	S	V	N
I	T	D	L	T	M	I	S	O	E	E	G
N	P	O	O	F	E	A	R	E	D	D	K
S	S	O	R	C	E	D	O	O	I	T	W
O	N	W	D	C	L	J	W	B	M	A	L

You have just discovered what the Hebrew name *Jehovah-jireh* means. Go back and look at verse 14. WHAT did Abraham name that place? _____

Isn't it awesome to know that God is Jehovah-jireh, our Provider? "In the mount of the LORD it will be provided." God takes care of all our needs. God provided a ram for Abraham to sacrifice in the place of his son Isaac.

Did you notice how Abraham offering up his only son is a picture of what God did for us? Tomorrow we are going to take a closer look at the Lord our Provider to discover just what God was willing to sacrifice for you and me.

OPERATION PROVISION

OK, GSAs, it's time for another martial arts lesson. But before Mr. Tim arrives, we need to pull out our Operations Manuals and continue to look at Jehovah-jireh, the Lord our Provider. Yesterday as we looked at the first time God's name Jehovah-jireh was used, we saw God provide a ram for Abraham to sacrifice in the place of his son Isaac.

Today let's find out WHAT God has provided for you and me. Look up and read John 3:16,17.

John 3:16 WHOM did God provide as a sacrifice?

_____

WHY did God provide this sacrifice?

_____

If we believe in Jesus, WHAT will we have?

_____

John 3:17 WHY did God send Jesus into the world?

_____

Now look up and read John 1:29 in your Operations Manual.

WHAT did John say when he saw Jesus coming to him?
"Behold, the _____ of _____ who takes
away the _____ of the world!"

Isaac was Abraham's promised son, and Jesus was God's promised Son. Isaac carried his own wood for the sacrifice, just like Jesus carried the cross that He was sacrificed on. And God provided a ram to take Isaac's place, while Jesus was the Lamb that was sacrificed in our place to pay for our sins.

Do you see just how much God loves you? He willingly gave up His only begotten Son to die in your place so that you would not perish, so you would not have to live forever in the

lake of fire prepared for the devil and his angels. God provided Jesus, the Lamb of God, to die in our place to pay for our sins. God provided a way of escape for you and me.

Did you know that a burnt offering was a voluntary offering? It was an offering that was made in love as an act of worship. In Genesis 22 we see Abraham offering Isaac as a burnt offering.

Now use your Operations Manual to read Leviticus 1 and find out more about the burnt offering.

Leviticus 1:4 WHAT was the burnt offering for?

A _ _ _ _ _ _ _ t (a covering for sin)

Just as a burnt offering is done voluntarily for atonement, Jesus willingly laid His life on the altar to be sacrificed and make atonement for you and me.

Is eternal life the only provision that God makes for us? Let's find out. Read Matthew 6:11 printed out below. This verse is part of the prayer that Jesus used to teach His disciples how to pray.

Give us this day our daily bread.

WHAT is Jesus teaching His disciples to pray for in this verse?

_____

God's name is Jehovah-jireh. This means we are to come to God to ask Him to meet our needs each and every day!

Now read Philippians 4:19 printed out below.

And my God will supply all your needs according to His riches in glory in Christ Jesus.

WHAT will God supply?

_____

Not only does God Jehovah-jireh provide for our eternal salvation, but He also provides for all of our daily needs! Isn't that fantastic? The Ruler of the universe loves and cares for you so much that He will provide for your every need. All you have to do is ask.

Before you head out to take your martial arts lesson, let's take a few more minutes to review all that we have learned about God's names. Draw a picture in each box on the next two pages to help you remember each one of these seven names of God that you have discovered. Write out what the name means. For example, under the name Elohim write out "God our Creator." Then draw a picture to remind you that God is your Creator.

You could draw a picture of the world for God as Creator, a throne with a crown over it for God Most High, eyes for a God who sees, a strong arm for God Almighty, a picture of you surrendering to God as Lord and Master, a burning bush for Jehovah the self-existent One and the I AM, and a cross as a picture of the Lord our Provider. Use your imagination and have fun as you remind yourself of WHO your God is!

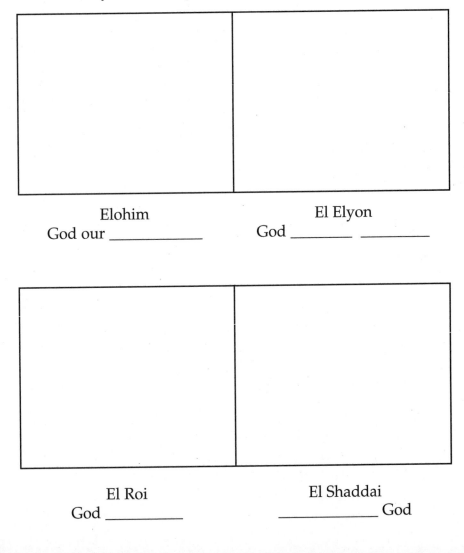

Elohim
God our _____

El Elyon
God _____ _____

El Roi
God _____

El Shaddai
_____ God

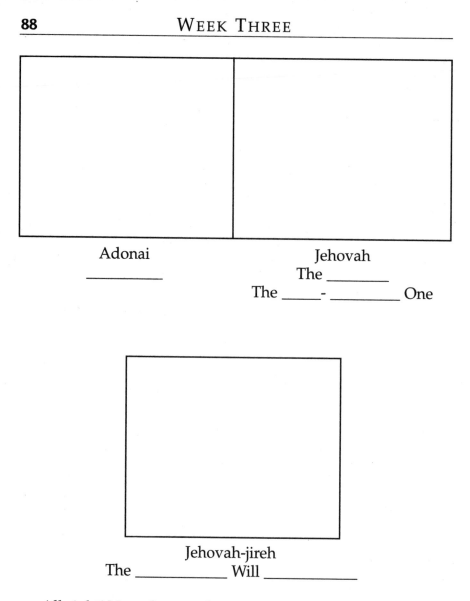

Adonai

_____

Jehovah

The _____

The _____ - _____ One

Jehovah-jireh

The _____ Will _____

All right! Now that you have seen just how awesome your God is, go outside and practice those special moves with Mr. Tim. And don't forget to say your verse out loud to a grown-up!

4

TACTICAL MOVEMENT UNDER GOD'S BANNER

Let's see, you have your tents, flashlights, compass, binoculars, paintball equipment, food, water, and most importantly, your Operations Manual and top secret notebook. It looks like you are ready for our next secret mission. Let's head into the woods with Uncle Matt for a special field training assignment that will help us uncover more about God's names and prepare us to be God's secret agents.

OUT IN THE FIELD

"What have you found so far?" Colby asked Max as they tromped through Uncle Matt's herb garden and fields looking for the plants listed in their notebooks.

"Let's see, I have something poisonous, and a few things that can be eaten, but I need to find a plant that can be used for medicine. Hey, Molly," Max called out, "have you and Ruthi found the herbs for healing?"

"I think so," Molly replied as she and Ruthi met up with Max and Colby to show them their finds.

As they looked through their containers, Max reminded them, "Uncle Matt said it's very important for agents in the field to be able to recognize which plants can be used for food and medicine. Let's head back to the campsite and see what Uncle Matt thinks about our finds."

Uncle Matt sat by the tent and examined each plant as he asked the kids to tell him which plants they could eat, which ones were poisonous, and which ones could be used for medicine. "You did a great job. It looks like you found at least one of each kind. Now why don't you search around the campsite to see if you can find the next secret message that will reveal one of God's names?"

A few minutes later, Colby shouted, "I found it! It was taped to the bottom of my canteen."

"All right," Uncle Matt replied. "Good work! Open it and let's see if you can figure it out."

Colby open the envelope to reveal this message:

GBELSE   OXMEX

"How do we crack this code, Uncle Matt?" Max asked.

Uncle Matt answered, "In this secret code you need to take the message and run down the alphabet with each letter of the message until you come to a word that is not gibberish. Like this: WHAT letter of the alphabet comes after the letter G which is the first letter in our message? H. So I will line the H up under the G like this:

G

H

I

and continue to the next letter I. Then I will line the letter I up under the letter H like it is above. I would continue to do this for about five letters, and then I would start running the second letter in the secret message, which is a B. So I would line up a C under my B and continue doing this until I had run all the letters in the secret message.

"After I had done this, then I would look at the letters I had run down to see if I can find any recognizable words. Check it out below. Look at the secret message and the letters that we have run underneath the message. Do you see any recognizable words as we run down the alphabet for each letter?"

WHAT line are the words in? _____ Now circle the words. Secret message:

GBELSE   OXMEX

HCFMTF   PYNFY

IDGNUG   QZOGZ

JEHOVAH   RAPHA

KFIPWBI   SBQIB

You have just broken another secret code. But what if a recognizable word did not appear after just five lines? Then you would just keep running the alphabet until you reached the end of the alphabet to find the words in your secret message.

WHAT does this name *Jehovah-rapha* (pronounced *je-HOE-vah RAH-fah*) mean? Let's find out. Read Exodus 15:22-26 printed out below.

> **22** Then Moses led Israel from the Red Sea, and they went out into the wilderness of Shur; and they went three days in the wilderness and found no water. **23** When they came to Marah, they could not drink the waters of Marah, for they were bitter; therefore it was named Marah. **24** So the people grumbled at Moses, saying, "What shall we drink?" **25** Then he cried out to the LORD, and the LORD showed him a tree; and he threw it into the waters, and the waters became sweet. There He

made for them a statute and regulation, and there
He tested them. **26** And He said, "If you will give
earnest heed to the voice of the LORD your God, and
do what is right in His sight, and give ear to His
commandments, and keep all His statutes, I will
put none of the diseases on you which I have put
on the Egyptians; for I, the LORD, am your healer."

Now gather the intel.

Exodus 15:25 WHAT was Moses' cure for the bitter
waters of Marah?
WHAT did Moses do?

_____

Look up and read Exodus 13:21,22. WHO was going
before them and leading the way on their journey?

_____

Was it an accident that the people ended up at Marah?

_____

Do you think the bitter waters at Marah were an accident? _____
WHY? _____

_____

Go back to the passage on page 91 on Exodus 15.
Exodus 15:25 WHAT did the Lord do when Moses cried
out to Him?

_____

WHAT happened to the waters?

_____

WHAT else did God do there?

He _____ them.

Exodus 15:26 WHAT would keep the people healthy?

_____

_____

WHO put the diseases on WHOM?

_____ put the diseases on the

_____.

WHAT do we see about the Lord?

_____

Did you get it? Do you know the meaning of God's name Jehovah-rapha? It means "the Lord is our Healer." Isn't it wonderful? God is the One we need to run to when we need healing.

Do you remember what we saw about God as we looked at Him as El Elyon, Most High God? Look up and read Deuteronomy 32:39 again.

WHO wounds? _____ WHO heals?

_____

Remember what we learned. God allows us to be wounded, but He is also the One who heals. God may lead us to bitter waters. Bitter waters are the hard times in life when someone we love is hurting, when someone says something mean and unkind that hurts our feelings, when things don't go our way or turn out the way we wanted them to. Even though God leads us to bitter waters, He is also the One who makes our bitter waters sweet. He is our Healer.

WHAT does God heal? We will find out tomorrow as we continue this special mission. But before we cook our dinner over the open campfire, you need to discover this week's memory verse. Uncle Matt has used a Key Word Secret Code with *Jehovah-rapha* as our key word to help discover this week's verse. Use the answer key below to help you decipher the code.

KEY WORD SECRET CODE

J E H O V A R P B C D F G I K L M N Q S T U W X Y Z
A B C D E F G H I J K L M N O P Q R S T U V W X Y Z

PVJF   GV,   K FKNO, JIO B   WBFF   EV

_____ _____ __ _____ _____ __ _____ _____

PVJFVO; QJUV GV JIO B WBFF EV

_____ _____ _____ _____ __ _____ _____

QJUVO, AKN   YKT JNV GY LNJBQV.

_____ _____ _____ _____ _____ _____

CVNVGBJP 17:14

_____

Now practice this verse out loud three times in a row, three times today!

OPERATION HEALING

Are you ready for another day of tromping through the woods, developing your self-preservation skills? Great! But before we head out, we need to pull out our Operations Manual to uncover more intel on Jehovah-rapha. Don't forget to pray!

Now let's look at some verses that will show us WHAT our Jehovah-rapha heals. Read 2 Chronicles 7:14 printed on the next page.

*And [if] My people who are called by My name humble
themselves and pray and seek My face and turn from
their wicked ways, then I will hear from heaven, will
forgive their sin and will heal their land.*

WHAT will God heal? _____

Does our land (our country) need healing? _____

WHAT do God's people need to do so that God will
heal?

_____

WHY? WHAT have they done? They have s __ __ __ __ d.

WHAT can we do so that God will heal our land? First
we need to turn from our wicked ways. Then we need to
pray that the people in our country will turn from their
sin and seek God.

Now read Psalm 147:3 printed out below.

He heals the brokenhearted and binds up their wounds.

WHOM does God heal? _____

WHAT does He do?

_____

Isn't that awesome to know that God loves you so much
that He not only binds up your wounds, but He will also heal
your broken heart?

Now read Psalm 103:1-3 printed out below.

1 Bless the Lord, O my soul, and all that is within
me, bless His holy name. **2** Bless the Lord, O my
soul, and forget none of His benefits; **3** who par-
dons all your iniquities, who heals all your diseases.

WHAT does God heal? _____

WHAT does He pardon? _____

Read 1 Peter 2:24,25 printed below.

> **24** And He Himself bore our sins in His body on
> the cross, so that we might die to sin and live to
> righteousness; for by His wounds you were
> healed. **25** For you were continually straying like
> sheep, but now you have returned to the Shepherd
> and Guardian of your souls.

WHAT are we healed from? WHAT are we to die to?

_____

HOW were we healed?

_____

To WHOM have we returned?

_____

Amazing! God allowed His precious Son to be wounded
so that we can be healed. Can you believe it? Did you see all
that God heals? He heals our land, our sickness, our broken
hearts, and our sin. He heals us physically, spiritually, and
emotionally. There is nothing in your life that Jehovah-rapha
cannot heal. But HOW? WHAT do you need to do?

First you need to run to God because He is your Healer.

Next you need to examine your heart to see if there is sin
in your life. Did you notice that in 2 Chronicles 7:14 God tells
them to turn from their wicked ways? And in 1 Peter 2:24 we
see that we are to die to sin and live to righteousness. God is
our Healer, but before He will heal us, we need to take care of

our sin. Do you know how to do that? Read Psalm 139:23,24 printed out below.

> **23** Search me, O God, and know my heart; try me and know my anxious thoughts; **24** and see if there be any hurtful way in me, and lead me in the everlasting way.

We need to ask God to search our hearts to see if there is any hurtful way that would cause sin in our life. WHAT do we do if we discover sin? Look up and read 1 John 1:9. If we confess our sins, God is faithful. He will forgive us our sins and cleanse us from all unrighteousness. Did you notice in Psalm 103:3 that pardoning our iniquities (our sins) comes before God's healing?

Now does this mean that all sickness comes because we sin? In a way, yes, because until man sinned in the Garden of Eden in Genesis 3, there was no sickness, pain, or death. But all sickness does not come from our personal sin. Some illnesses can have other causes. Look up and read John 9:1-3.

Did anyone sin to make this man blind? _____

Look at verse 3. WHY was this man blind?

_____

Sometimes God uses our sickness and our wounds for His glory so that others can see WHO He is and come to know Him.

Are you hurting? Do you remember what you learned in Romans 8:28? God causes all things to work together for good. That includes our broken hearts, our wounds, our sickness, and the sin in our land.

God is our Healer. Only He can take the bitter waters, those hard times and difficult situations in our lives, and make them sweet. God will heal us if we will just run to Him.

WHY don't you practice saying your memory verse out loud? As you do, give God all the praise and thank Him for sending His Son to be wounded to take away your sin so that you can be healed!

RAISING THE BANNER

"Are you ready to capture the flag?" Uncle Matt asked as he came out of his tent.

"You better believe it," Colby answered.

"Then let's go over the rules. Max and Molly are on the Alpha team. You will use orange paint. Ruthi and Colby, you will be on the Bravo team, and your paintballs will be blue. Your mission is to capture the flag at the fort and return it to home base. If the other team shoots you with their paintball gun and it marks you with their paint color, then you have to drop the flag and fall down. The first member of the team to arrive at home base with the flag wins."

"This is going to be great!" Max smiled as he loaded his paintball gun.

"Then head out," replied Uncle Matt. "You have five minutes, which will be 0800 hours, to get into position before the battle begins. I will be monitoring the battle with my binoculars and will meet both teams back at home base." Thirty minutes later a paint-splattered Max and Colby arrived back at home base to see Molly waving the flag. "Yippee, we did it!" Max shouted. "Way to go, Molly. I see our ambush worked, and you made it back safely."

"I sure did," Molly laughed. "But Ruthi saw me as I was crossing the creek. She hit the tree but missed me."

Uncle Matt chuckled as he looked at Max and Colby. Max was covered in blue paint, while Colby was splattered with orange. "It doesn't look like these two escaped unharmed. You two must have had quite an adventure. You'll have to share it with me at lunch."

"We sure did," Colby laughed. "I don't know who got hit first."

"OK, now that the flag has been captured," Uncle Matt said, "let's take a look at the two encoded words on the flag to discover God's name."

JHVHIS-EOANSI

"Now," Uncle Matt explained, "this is a zigzag code. A zigzag message is written by alternating the letters of the message you want to send with the top and bottom lines like this:

J   H   V   H   I   S

E   O   A   N   S   I

"The top line is written like it is one word, and the second line is written like it is another word. You put a dash between the two words to separate them so you will know how to write it out like it is above.

"Next you take a pen and connect the letters with a zigzag line like this: J   H   V   H   I   S

E   O   A   N   S   I

"Now decode it. *J* connects to *E* and *E* to *H* and so forth. Put these letters together top to bottom to discover God's name. Write it out on the lines below."

_____ - _____

Let's uncover the meaning of this name of God, *Jehovah-nissi* (pronounced *je-HOE-vah NIS-see*). Turn to page 184 to your Observation Worksheet on Exodus 17. Read Exodus 17:8-16 and mark the following key words:

Israel (draw a blue star of David)

Amalek (color it orange)

Lord (draw a purple triangle and color it yellow)

staff (draw a brown staff)

Mark anything that tells you WHERE by double-underlining the WHERE in green. And don't forget to mark anything that tells you WHEN by drawing a green clock like this:

Now before we gather the intel, do you know WHERE Amalek comes from? Abraham had a son named Isaac who had two sons, Esau and Jacob. Esau was the firstborn and should have been the rightful heir to Isaac, but because Esau despised his birthright and sold it for a bowl of pottage (stew), Jacob received the birthright.

Esau had a son named Eliphaz, and Eliphaz was the father of Amalek. Amalek was Esau's grandson, a direct descendant of Isaac. Amalek was also the first and constant enemy of Israel. After the children of Israel came out of Egypt and crossed the Red Sea by the mighty salvation of the Lord (Exodus 14:13), and after they had eaten bread from heaven and had drunk water from the rock, the very first enemy they had to deal with was Amalek.

Now that we have our background information, let's gather the intel.

Exodus 17:8 WHERE does Amalek fight Israel? _____

Exodus 17:9 WHERE does Moses station himself?

_____

WHAT does Moses hold in his hand?

_____

Did you know that the staff was a symbol of the power
of God?
Exodus 17:11 WHAT happened when Moses held up his
hand?

_____

WHAT happened when Moses put his hand down?

_____

Exodus 17:12 WHAT happened to Moses' hands?

_____

WHAT did Aaron and Hur do?

_____

Exodus 17:13 WHO won the battle?

_____

Exodus 17:15 WHAT did Moses name the altar?

_____

That's what *Jehovah-nissi* means: "The LORD Is My Banner"!
WHAT is a banner? Do you know? A banner was a standard.
In ancient times sometimes a banner was a pole with an orna-
ment that glittered in the sun. Today a banner is like a flag.
The banner was carried out front, ahead of the soldiers, to
indicate the line of march or the rallying point on the battle-
field.

In Exodus 17 we see that when Israel fought against Amalek, Moses held God's staff up and Israel prevailed. But when he grew tired and put down God's staff, Israel started losing.

After the fight was over and Israel had won, Moses built an altar and named it The Lord Is My Banner to show that the battle was the Lord's. Victory came when the Lord was lifted up. This name of God shows us that God goes before us in battle just like the banner goes before the soldiers.

> Take a look at the last verse in Exodus 17. WHAT did the Lord swear?
>
> _____

Is there going to be a constant battle with Amalek? Yes! HOW does this apply to us? WHAT do we do when we come up against our enemy (the devil), since we have discovered that the Lord is our banner? We will find out tomorrow as we take a look at how we are to raise our banner and fight!

ON THE ALERT—DEFEAT THE ENEMY

How did you like our paintball battle yesterday? It was a lot of messy fun. Uncle Matt is going to let us go back in the field for another game of Capture the Flag today. Colby and Ruthi are determined to capture it this time. And we're going to let Sam go out in the open, too, to see if he can escape from becoming an orange-and-blue beagle! But before we put on our gear and head out, we need to finish the mission we started yesterday. WHAT do we do when our enemy comes against us? Let's find out. Read Ephesians 6:10-18 printed out on the next page and mark the two key phrases and the key word listed here:

（put on the full armor of God）(circle it in blue)

stand firm (box it in orange)

devil (draw a red pitchfork)

Ephesians 6:10-18

10 Finally, be strong in the Lord and in the strength of His might. **11** Put on the full armor of God, so that you will be able to stand firm against the schemes of the devil. **12** For our struggle is not against flesh and blood, but against the rulers, against the powers, against the world forces of this darkness, against the spiritual forces of wickedness in the heavenly places. **13** Therefore, take up the full armor of God, so that you will be able to resist in the evil day, and having done everything, to stand firm. **14** Stand firm therefore, having girded your loins with truth, and having put on the breastplate of righteousness, **15** and having shod your feet with the preparation of the gospel of peace; **16** in addition to all, taking up the shield of faith with which you will be able to extinguish all the flaming arrows of the evil one. **17** And take the helmet of salvation, and the sword of the Spirit, which is the word of God. **18** With all prayer and petition pray at all times in the Spirit, and with this in view, be on the alert with all perseverance and petition for all the saints.

Ephesians 6:10 WHAT is the first thing we are to do?

_____

Ephesians 6:11 WHAT are we to put on?

_____

WHY?

_____

Ephesians 6:12 As Christians, against WHAT do we struggle?
Is our battle against flesh and blood? _____
List WHAT our battle is against.

_____

_____

_____

_____

Ephesians 6:13 HOW are we to stand? _____
Ephesians 6:14 WHAT are you to gird your loins with?

_____

WHAT kind of breastplate are you to put on?

_____

Ephesians 6:15 WHAT are you to put on your feet?

_____

Ephesians 6:16 WHAT kind of shield do you put on?

_____

WHAT does the shield do?

_____

Ephesians 6:17 WHAT is the helmet?

_____

WHAT is the sword of the Spirit?

_____

Ephesians 6:18 WHAT are we to do at all times?

_____

   When we come against the enemy, we are not to surrender. We are to put on the armor of God, raise our banner, and fight. Jehovah-nissi is our banner. We are to be strong in the Lord and in the strength of His might.
   Let's practice putting on our armor. Draw a soldier in the box below. Now add each piece of armor as we come to it.

   Gird your loins with truth. Soldiers used a belt around their waist to gird their loins. Draw the belt of truth on your soldier. How can we put on the belt of truth? By studying God's Word every day, just like you are doing right now.
   Put on the breastplate of righteousness. Draw a breastplate on your soldier. Soldiers wore the breastplate to protect their vital organs, such as their heart, lungs, stomach, and kidneys, so the enemy's arrows could not get through and kill them. Protect yourself with the breastplate of righteousness. God

always does the right thing, and that's what He wants us to do. We can do the right thing by staying away from sin and doing what God says in His Word. Then the enemy can't touch us!

Make sure your feet are shod with the preparation of the gospel of peace. Draw some sandals on your soldier's feet to represent the gospel of peace. In Roman times the sandals weren't slick on the bottom. They had "grippers" so people could stand firm and not be shaken. When you know that you belong to God, then there is a peace in your heart. You are on God's side and He is on yours, and the devil can't win against God. You can stand firm!

Take up the shield of faith. Draw the shield on your soldier. This shield enabled the soldier to put out the flaming arrows that were shot at him. The shield was made of leather and soaked in water so when those fiery missiles came at a soldier, they would sizzle out when they hit the shield.

Whenever the enemy throws a lie or a doubt or an accusation at you, just hold up the Word and say, "But God says," and then give the devil a verse that counteracts the lie. Remember, this is the way Jesus won against the devil when He was tempted in the wilderness. The more you know God's Word, the stronger your shield will be. Soak your shield in the water of God's Word every day, just like you are doing right now, and the enemy won't be able to get to you.

Take the helmet of salvation. Draw a helmet on your soldier. Soldiers wore this on their head to protect their head from deadly blows. We need to protect our minds by remembering to whom we belong. Christ lives inside of Christians, and He is stronger than the enemy. Greater is He who is in you than he (the devil and his cohorts) who is in the world. Keep your helmet on!

Draw the sword of the Spirit. The sword of the Spirit is God's Word. It is our only offensive weapon because it is all we need for victory.

The only way we can fight is with God's Word. Pull that sword out of its sheath and use it!

You did it! Now as you head back into the field to play Capture the Flag, practice putting your armor on so that you can win the battle every day of your life. Remember, the Lord is your banner. We can only prevail when the Lord is lifted up!

GOD'S PLAN OF ACTION

"Hey, Uncle Matt, what's for breakfast?" Max asked as he walked up to the campfire.

"How about we head to the lake and see if we can catch some fish for our breakfast, since this is our last day out in the field?"

"That sounds great. I'll go find the rest of the team so we can get started."

"Mmmmmm! This fish is so good," Molly sighed as she finished the last bite. "Why does everything taste so much better when you're camping?"

"It's because you work so hard to get it," Colby answered.

As Max rubbed Sam, he noticed something under his collar. "Hey, Sam, old boy, what's this?" Max asked as he pulled out a folded piece of paper. "Hey, it's another secret message."

"All right!" exclaimed Colby.

OK, GSAs, grab your codebooks and find out what this message reveals to us about God's name. It looks like Uncle Matt has used another number cipher, but this one is a little bit different. Take a look at Sam's secret message below.

17-22-19-12-5-26-19   14-22-16-12-23-23-18-8-19-16-22-14

_____   _____

Find the letter of the alphabet that matches the number in the code by looking at our Number Cipher Secret Code below. Now go back and write the correct letters that match the numbers on the lines under the encoded message.

NUMBER CIPHER SECRET CODE

A	B	C	D	E	F	G	H	I	J	K	L	M	N
26	25	24	23	22	21	20	19	18	17	16	15	14	13

O	P	Q	R	S	T	U	V	W	X	Y	Z
12	11	10	9	8	7	6	5	4	3	2	1

Awesome! Another code name for God is revealed: *Jehovah-mekoddishkem* (pronounced *je-HOE-vah me-KAH-dish-KEM*). Now WHAT does this code name for God reveal about His character? Let's find out. First let's put ourselves in context. God reveals this name to Moses after the children of Israel leave Rephidim and come to the wilderness of Sinai and camp in the wilderness in front of the mountain.

Now read Exodus 31:12-18 printed out on page 109 and mark the following key words:

sabbath (circle it in blue)

sign (draw a red sign)

holy (draw a purple cloud and color it yellow)

death (draw a black tombstone and color it brown)

covenant (box it in yellow and color it red)

Don't forget to mark anything that tells you WHERE by double-underlining the WHERE in green. And don't forget to mark anything that tells you WHEN by drawing a green clock like this:

Exodus 31:12-18

12 The LORD spoke to Moses, saying, **13** "But as for you, speak to the sons of Israel, saying, `You shall surely observe My sabbaths; for this is a sign between Me and you throughout your generations, that you may know that I am the LORD who sanctifies you. **14** Therefore you are to observe the sabbath, for it is holy to you. Everyone who profanes it shall surely be put to death; for whoever does any work on it, that person shall be cut off from among his people. **15** For six days work may be done, but on the seventh day there is a sabbath of complete rest, holy to the LORD; whoever does any work on the sabbath day shall surely be put to death. **16** So the sons of Israel shall observe the sabbath, to celebrate the sabbath throughout their generations as a perpetual covenant.' **17** It is a sign between Me and the sons of Israel forever; for in six days the LORD made heaven and earth, but on the seventh day He ceased from labor, and was refreshed." **18** When He had finished speaking with him upon Mount Sinai, He gave Moses the two tablets of the testimony, tablets of stone, written by the finger of God.

Now gather the information. WHO is Jehovah-mekod-dishkem?

Exodus 31:13 WHAT are the sons of Israel to observe?

_____

WHY? _____

WHAT is this sign to show them about the Lord?

_____

This is the meaning of the name *Jehovah-mekoddishkem:* "The Lord Who Sanctifies You." WHAT does it mean to be sanctified? This word means "to be made holy, to be set apart." The Lord is telling Moses that He is the Lord who makes them holy, who sets them apart.

WHAT does the Lord want them to do to remind them of WHO He is? WHAT does He want the children of Israel to observe?

_____

Exodus 31:15 WHAT is the sabbath?

_____

WHAT will happen to the person who works on the sabbath? _____

Exodus 31:16 HOW long are they to celebrate the sabbath?

_____

Exodus 31:17 WHAT was their example? WHAT did the Lord do?

_____

The Lord gave the sabbath as a sign so that the children of Israel would know that the Lord was the One who set them apart and made them holy. Each and every week as they celebrated the sabbath they would be reminded of WHO God is and WHO they were to God. Look up and read 1 Peter 2:9.

WHAT are the children of Israel, according to this verse?

_____

Now that we have seen that the Lord is the One who sanctifies us, let's find out how we receive our sanctification. HOW are we set apart and made holy? Read Hebrews 10:10-14 printed out below.

> **10** By this will we have been sanctified through the offering of the body of Jesus Christ once for all. **11** Every priest stands daily ministering and offering time after time the same sacrifices, which can never take away sins; **12** but He, having offered one sacrifice for sins for all time, sat down at the right hand of God, **13** waiting from that time onward until His enemies be made a footstool for His feet. **14** For by one offering He has perfected for all time those who are sanctified.

Hebrews 10:10 HOW are we sanctified?

_____

When Jesus died on the cross and paid for our sins, He set us apart and made us holy. There is absolutely nothing we can do to make ourselves holy. God's name shows us it's about God. The Lord is the One who sanctifies.

When we receive Jesus Christ as our Savior and God saves us, then He sets us apart and makes us holy. It is a gift of God and not of works (Ephesians 2:8,9). After we have been saved and sanctified, then we will want to live a holy life by studying God's Word and doing what He says is right. We will want to be imitators of God (Ephesians 5:1,2).

Are you doing that? You are studying God's Word right now. But are you doing what God says is right in His Word?

_____

Are you walking in purity (1 Thessalonians 4:2-4)? Are you watching what you see, what you think, what you do with your hands and your body? Are you careful about the things that you say? Write out what you are doing.

_____

Can your friends see a difference in you from the other kids who are not living pure and holy lives? Being holy means to be set apart for God, which means to be set apart from sin. Are you different? Have you set yourself apart from sin? Write out on the line below if you have set yourself apart, if there is a difference in you.

_____

Just remember that the Lord is Jehovah-mekoddishkem. He has set you apart and made you holy. Are you living the way your holy God would want you to?

5
CRISIS TRAINING—GOD'S DELIVERANCE

How did you like our field mission last week? It was a lot of fun tromping through the woods, having paintball battles, and fishing for our breakfast! But now it's back to the cabin. We have a lot more to learn as we continue to spy out truth and uncover God's code names.

A PEACEKEEPING MISSION

"Hey, Uncle Matt, we're back," Molly called out as she opened the cabin door.

"Hey, guys, I see you got my note. Are you ready for your scuba-diving lessons?"

"We can't wait!" Colby exclaimed.

"We'll head out right after we complete our next mission," said Uncle Matt. "Molly, did your mom tell you to bring the note that I sent?"

"She sure did. I have it right here."

"Why did you want Molly to bring the note, Uncle Matt, since you wrote it?" Max asked.

"Good question, Max. It's because the note is written in an open code. It contains one of God's Hebrew names."

"It does?" Max asked. "Can I see the note, Molly?" Molly handed Max the note, and they each looked it over. "I don't see it, Uncle Matt."

"That's what makes it a great secret code. It looks just like an ordinary letter with nothing to hide."

OK, GSAs, read Molly's note below.

Hi, Molly,

Just wanted to make sure that you will be at the cabin at 0900 hours. Everything is ready for your next mission. Have Ruthi bring a swimsuit. One of our activities will be diving in the lake. Van will be your diving instructor. All of you will get a chance to use the scuba equipment. Have you ever dived before? Sam is going to love the water. He can really dog paddle. Also don't forget your sunscreen. Last time Max got really sunburned. One more thing: Don't forget your water gun. Max wants to have a water battle after the scuba lesson.

See you at 0900,
Uncle Matt

Now, GSAs, crack the open code and discover God's name. Take the first letter of the first word at the beginning of each sentence and circle it. Now write these letters on the line below to spell out God's Hebrew name.

_____

Fantastic! You now know that God's name is Jehovah-shalom (pronounced *je-HOE-vah sha-LOAM*). WHAT does this name mean?

To reveal the secret of God's name, turn to your Observation Worksheet on page 186 and read Judges 6.

Now gather the intel to solve the crossword puzzle on page 116.

Judges 6:1 WHY did God give the sons of Israel into the hands of Midian for seven years?

1. (Down) Because the sons of _____ did what was

2. (Across) _____ in the sight of the Lord.

Judges 6:6 WHAT did the sons of Israel do after their land was devastated and they were brought low by the Midianites?

3. (Across) "The sons of Israel _____ to the

4. (Across) _____.

Judges 6:12 WHAT did the angel of the Lord say to Gideon?

5. (Across) "The LORD is _____ you, O valiant

6. (Across) _____."

Judges 6:14 WHAT did God tell Gideon to do?

7. (Down) "Go...and _____ Israel from the hand of Midian.

8. (Down) Have I not _____ you?"

Judges 6:17 WHAT did Gideon ask for so he would know that he had found favor in the Lord's sight and that it was the Lord speaking to Him?

9. (Down) "Show me a _____."

Judges 6:23 WHAT did the Lord say to Gideon after Gideon said he had seen the angel of the Lord face-to-face?

10. (Down) "Peace to you, do not _____; you shall not die."

Judges 6:24 WHAT did Gideon name the altar he built to the Lord?

11. (Down) The Lord is _____.

Jehovah-shalom means "The LORD is Peace." The only place we can truly find peace is in a right relationship with God. Just look at Gideon's dark and desperate situation. And yet in his darkest hours, God reveals Himself to Gideon as The Lord is Peace.

Now that we know that the Lord is peace, let's take a look at some other scriptures to see what we can learn about peace and its relationship to God.

Read Numbers 6:22-27 printed out below.

> **22** Then the LORD spoke to Moses, saying, **23** "Speak to Aaron and to his sons, saying, 'Thus you shall bless the sons of Israel. You shall say to them: **24** The LORD bless you, and keep you; **25** the LORD make His face shine on you, and be gracious to you; **26** the LORD lift up His countenance on you, and give you peace.' **27** So they shall invoke My name on the sons of Israel, and I then will bless them."

Numbers 6:26 WHAT will the Lord give us?

_____

Read Jeremiah 29:11 printed out below.

> *"For I know the plans that I have for you," declares the* LORD, *"plans for welfare and not for calamity to give you a future and a hope."*

WHAT are God's plans for us?

_____

Read Isaiah 26:3 printed out below.

> *The steadfast of mind You will keep in perfect peace, because he trusts in You.*

HOW can we have peace?

_____

Read Romans 5:1 printed out below.

> *Therefore, having been justified by faith, we have peace with God through our Lord Jesus Christ.*

HOW do we have peace with God?

_____

Read Philippians 4:8,9 printed out below.

> **8** Finally, brethren, whatever is true, whatever is honorable, whatever is right, whatever is pure, whatever is lovely, whatever is of good repute, if there is any excellence and if anything worthy of praise, dwell on these things. **9** The things you have learned and received and heard and seen in

me, practice these things, and the God of peace
will be with you.

WHAT do we need to dwell on to have God's peace?

_____

_____

Look up and read Isaiah 9:6.

WHO is Jesus? The _____ of _____

Now read Hebrews 13:5,6 printed out below.

> 5 "I will never desert you, nor will I ever forsake
> you," 6 so that we confidently say, "The LORD is
> my helper, I will not be afraid. What will man do
> to me?"

Hebrews 13:5 WHAT does Jesus promise us?

_____

Do we have to be afraid when hard times come? No! What
if someone tells you something about someone else, or you
hear something someone has said about you, or something
bad happens at home? It may be true, but is it worthy of
praise? We cannot let our minds dwell on the bad and hard
things in our lives. We have just seen that Jesus will give us
His perfect peace in spite of our circumstances. We are to
dwell on the things that are true, honorable, right, pure, love-
ly, of good repute, excellent, and worthy of praise. Our minds
are to stay on Him. The Lord has plans for us to give us a
future and a hope. He is our Helper. WHAT can man do to
us?

Now discover this week's memory verse that reminds
you to run to Jehovah-shalom and rest in Him. To decode
this verse, use the Inverse Alphabet Code by finding the letter

of the alphabet that represents the letter written in the encoded verse.

INVERSE ALPHABET CODE												
A	B	C	D	E	F	G	H	I	J	K	L	M	N
Z	Y	X	W	V	U	T	S	R	Q	P	O	N	M
O	P	Q	R	S	T	U	V	W	X	Y	Z	
L	K	J	I	H	G	F	E	D	C	B	A	

KVZXV R OVZEV DRGS BLF; NB KVZXV

_____ __ _____ ____ ___; __ _____

R TREV GL BLF; MLG ZH GSV DLIOW

_ ____ __ ___; ___ __ ___ _____

TREVH, WL R TREV GL BLF. WL MLG

_____, __ _ ____ __ ___. __ ___

OVG BLFI SVZIG YV GILFYOVW, MLI OVG

___ ____ _____ __ _____, ___ ___

RG YV UVZIUFO.

__ __ _____.

QLSM 14:27

_____

Way to go! Practice saying this verse out loud three times today.

TOP-SECRET DEVICE

"Hey, Uncle Matt," Max called out. "Look what I found outside the barn when we were putting our go-carts away."

"Wow, that's an Eisenhower silver dollar," Uncle Matt replied.

"Is it yours? I have already asked Molly, Colby, and Ruthi."

Uncle Matt smiled a sly grin as he replied, "Actually it is mine. I planted it out by the barn for one of you to find. Do you know what this really is?"

"You mean it's not a real silver dollar?" Colby asked.

"No, it's not. Remember, in the spy business things are rarely as they seem."

"But what is it, Uncle Matt?" Molly asked.

"This is a silver dollar hollow container made to look like a real Eisenhower silver dollar. It is used to hide secret messages or film without them being detected. It makes a great concealment device because it looks just like regular pocket change, which makes it virtually undetectable."

"Sweet!" Max and Colby yelled out at the same time.

"Go ahead, Max, and open it up. I believe there is a secret message inside that will reveal another one of God's names."

As Max opened the container, this is the message that he found inside.

ɿbvoɹɘL

ɿɈoodɒꙄ

"Hey," Colby cried out, "I know how to solve this secret message. All we need to do is hold it up to a mirror."

"Great work, Colby. Why don't you take this into the bedroom and hold it up to the mirror to discover God's name. Write it out in your top-secret notebook below."

_____ - _____

All right, GSAs, now that you have discovered God's name, let's pull out those Operations Manuals and get to work. WHAT does this name *Jehovah-sabaoth* (pronounced *je-HOE-vah SAH-bah-oath*) mean?

This name of God is not used until the book of 1 Samuel. First Samuel takes place in the final days of the judges, when there was great upheaval and distress in Israel. It was a time of darkness, insecurity, change, and constant conflict. It was a lot like our world is today!

Let's take a look at the first time this name Jehovah-sabaoth is used in 1 Samuel. Read 1 Samuel 1:1-11 printed out below.

> **1** Now there was a certain man from Ramathaim-zophim from the hill country of Ephraim, and his name was Elkanah the son of Jeroham, the son of Elihu, the son of Tohu, the son of Zuph, an Ephraimite. **2** He had two wives: the name of one was Hannah and the name of the other Peninnah; and Peninnah had children, but Hannah had no children. **3** Now this man would go up from his city yearly to worship and to sacrifice to the LORD of hosts in Shiloh. And the two sons of Eli, Hophni and Phinehas, were priests to the LORD there. **4** When the day came that Elkanah sacrificed, he would give portions to Peninnah his wife and to all her sons and her daughters; **5** but to Hannah he would give a double portion, for he loved Hannah, but the LORD had closed her womb. **6** Her rival, however, would provoke her bitterly to irritate her, because the LORD had closed her womb. **7** It happened year after year, as often as she went up to the house of the LORD, she would provoke her; so she wept and would not eat. **8** Then Elkanah her husband said to her, "Hannah, why do you weep and why do you not eat and why is your heart sad? Am I not better to you than ten sons?" **9** Then

Hannah rose after eating and drinking in Shiloh. Now Eli the priest was sitting on the seat by the doorpost of the temple of the LORD. **10** She, greatly distressed, prayed to the LORD and wept bitterly. **11** She made a vow and said, "O LORD of hosts, if You will indeed look on the affliction of Your maidservant and remember me, and not forget Your maidservant, but will give Your maidservant a son, then I will give him to the LORD all the days of his life, and a razor shall never come on his head."

Now gather the intel.

1 Samuel 1:2 WHO were Elkanah's two wives?

_____

WHAT do we see about his wife Hannah?

_____

Did you know that it was a disgrace in biblical times not to have any children? Children are a blessing from the Lord.

1 Samuel 1:3 WHO did Elkanah ("this man") worship and sacrifice to in Shiloh? _____

This is the meaning of God's name Jehovah-sabaoth. God is the Lord of hosts. This name shows God as our Deliverer. This is the name we run to when we have failed, when we are inadequate. When there is no other help, we have Jehovah-sabaoth, the Lord of hosts. We need to run to Him. He is our Deliverer.

1 Samuel 1:5 WHOM did Elkanah love?

_____

1 Samuel 1:6 WHAT would Elkanah's other wife, Hannah's rival, do to Hannah? _____

1 Samuel 1:7 HOW did Hannah respond?

_____

1 Samuel 1:10 WHAT did Hannah do in her great distress?

_____

1 Samuel 1:11 To WHOM did Hannah pray? WHAT name of God did she use? _____

Did you see to WHOM Hannah ran in her brokenness, when all hope was lost? She was so distressed that she knew her only hope was the Lord of hosts, her Deliverer. Did the Lord of hosts hear her cry of distress and answer? Take a look at 1 Samuel 1:19,20 below.

> **19** Then they arose early in the morning and worshiped before the LORD, and returned again to their house in Ramah. And Elkanah had relations with Hannah his wife, and the LORD remembered her. **20** It came about in due time, after Hannah had conceived, that she gave birth to a son; and she named him Samuel, saying, "Because I have asked him of the LORD."

1 Samuel 1:19 WHAT did the Lord do?

_____

1 Samuel 1:20 WHY did Hannah name him Samuel?

_____

Isn't it awesome to know that you have a God who will deliver you out of your affliction and distress? HOW about when you are in conflict and warfare with the enemy? We have already learned that Jehovah-nissi is our Banner who goes before us in battle. WHAT about Jehovah-sabaoth, the Lord of hosts, our Deliverer? Is this the name we should call on to fight our enemy? We will find out more tomorrow as we take a look at a young man named David, who had to face a giant enemy!

As you head out to do a little physical training, why don't you practice saying God's names? Do you remember all of them? Remember, secret agents need to memorize all important intel. To be God's secret agent, you definitely need to know His names. So get to work, GSAs. Keep practicing until you know all of God's names!

DEFEAT THE ENEMY

Yesterday you discovered that God is the LORD of hosts, Jehovah-sabaoth, our Deliverer. As we continue to look at this awesome name of God today, did you know that this is the name that David called on in battle as he stood alone against Goliath?

David was an untrained, young shepherd boy who went into battle against a Philistine giant named Goliath. David was unarmed except for a stick in his hand, five smooth stones, and his sling (1 Samuel 17:40). Goliath was a nine-foot-tall armed warrior. If you read 1 Samuel 17:5-7, you can see what Goliath wore into battle. WHAT would you have done if you found yourself standing before this armed giant? Let's find out WHAT David does. Read 1 Samuel 17:42-47 printed out on the next page.

42 When the Philistine looked and saw David, he disdained him; for he was but a youth, and ruddy, with a handsome appearance. **43** The Philistine said to David, "Am I a dog, that you come to me with sticks?" And the Philistine cursed David by his gods. **44** The Philistine also said to David, "Come to me, and I will give your flesh to the birds of the sky and the beasts of the field." **45** Then David said to the Philistine, "You come to me with a sword, a spear, and a javelin, but I come to you in the name of the LORD of hosts, the God of the armies of Israel, whom you have taunted. **46** This day the LORD will deliver you up into my hands, and I will strike you down and remove your head from you. And I will give the dead bodies of the army of the Philistines this day to the birds of the sky and the wild beasts of the earth, that all the earth may know that there is a God in Israel, **47** and that all this assembly may know that the LORD does not deliver by sword or by spear; for the battle is the LORD's and He will give you into our hands."

1 Samuel 17:43 WHAT did the Philistine (Goliath) say to David?

_____

1 Samuel 17:45 HOW did David respond? HOW did David come to the Philistine?

_____

1 Samuel 17:46 WHAT is the LORD going to do?

_____

WHAT will everyone in all the earth know?

_____

1 Samuel 17:47 To WHOM does the battle belong?

Isn't this fantastic? You don't have to worry or be afraid. The battle does not belong to you. It belongs to the LORD! Did you know that He is the LORD over all the armies of heaven? The name *sabaoth* means "a mass." It refers to a mass of heavenly beings, a mass of angels, or an army of the heavenly hosts. We do not have to fear our enemy because we can call on the LORD, who rules over all the armies of heaven. WHO is your enemy? _____ Do you remember what you learned about him in Week Two, Day Two, pages 45–48 as you looked at God Most High, El Elyon? You saw that God has all the power, and that He is the One who gave Satan permission to touch Job and sift Peter like wheat.

WHAT else did you see in Week Four, Day Four, on pages 102–04 as we looked at Ephesians 6:12? Against WHOM is our struggle as Christians? Is it against flesh and blood? _____ It's against the rulers, against the powers, against the world forces of this darkness, against the spiritual forces of wickedness in the heavenly places. Our enemy also uses people (Ephesians 2:2), the sons of disobedience, to come against the Lord's children. That's why we need to know God as Jehovah-sabaoth because only He can deliver us from our enemy. He is the Lord of all powers, principalities, and rulers in high places.

Isn't that awesome? The battle isn't yours. It's the Lord's! You can trust Him because He is Jehovah-sabaoth, LORD of hosts. He is El Elyon, the sovereign, most high God. And He is Jehovah-nissi, your Banner of victory! All you need to do is call on His name.

Can you treat God's name as "magic"—simply call on His name and expect Him to perform—if you don't have a relationship with Him where you walk with Him and obey Him? Let's take another look at Proverbs 18:10.

The name of the LORD is a strong tower; the righteous runs into it and is safe.

For WHOM is the strong tower of God's name? WHO is safe?

_____

Remember, to be righteous is to be made right with God and to do what God says is right. God's name isn't to be used like magic. When we have a right relationship with God, then God will hear and deliver us. We can run to Him as our refuge. His name is a strong tower. We will be safe!

Sing to the LORD, praise the LORD! For He has delivered the soul of the needy one from the hand of evildoers (Jeremiah 20:13).

CONTACTING OUR SOURCE

"Hey, guys," Uncle Matt said as Max, Molly, Sam, Colby, and Ruthi sat on the deck. "Are you ready to make another contact?"

"Yes!" Max responded.

"OK, this is your mission. You need to go to the zoo. Go and look at the monkeys, then head to the concession stand to the right. Max, this time it will be your turn to make contact. You need to wear your Clemson baseball hat. Walk up to the man working the concession stand and ask for a Cherry Coke. After he gives it to you, ask him if you can have three quarters for a dollar."

"But, Uncle Matt," Max interrupted, "shouldn't he give me four quarters for a dollar?"

"Yes, but that's how he will know you are his contact. The Clemson hat, Cherry Coke, and three quarters are his signal to tell you how to discover the next secret message. When he hands you the quarters, he will tell you what to do next. Are you ready to move out? Then hop on those bikes and head to the zoo."

As the man at the concession stand handed Max his cherry Coke, Max asked him if he would give him three quarters for a dollar.

"Yes," the man replied and handed Max the money. "You might want to feed the deer today," the man continued. "There's a feeding machine right over there. It takes quarters."

"What happened?" Molly asked as Max headed back.

"He told me to feed the deer and pointed to that feeding machine."

"All right!" Colby exclaimed. "Let's check it out."

Max put his quar-  ter in, turned the handle, and opened the door to find another secret message. "Cool! Here it is. Let's hop on our bikes and race to the cabin so we can decode it."

All right, GSAs, now it's your turn. Find out God's name.

KFIPWBI-SBBI

_____ - _____

To decode this secret message, GSAs, you need to choose the letter of the alphabet that comes before the letter that is written in code. Do this for each letter in the secret message until you have discovered God's name.

ALPHABET CODE													
A	B	C	D	E	F	G	H	I	J	K	L	M	N
O	P	Q	R	S	T	U	V	W	X	Y	Z		

Now that we uncovered God's name Jehovah-raah (pronounced *je-HOE-vah RAH-ah*), let's spy out what this name means. Read Psalm 23 printed out below.

> **1** The LORD is my shepherd, I shall not want. **2** He makes me lie down in green pastures; He leads me beside quiet waters. **3** He restores my soul; He guides me in the paths of righteousness for His name's sake. **4** Even though I walk through the valley of the shadow of death, I fear no evil, for You are with me; Your rod and Your staff, they comfort me. **5** You prepare a table before me in the presence of my enemies; You have anointed my head with oil; my cup overflows. **6** Surely goodness and lovingkindness will follow me all the days of my life, and I will dwell in the house of the LORD forever.

Psalm 23:1 WHAT is the Lord?

_____

This is the meaning of God's name Jehovah-raah. Since the Lord is our Shepherd, WHAT does that make us? Look up and read the following verses in your Operations Manual, the Bible.

Isaiah 53:6 To WHAT are we being compared? _____

Psalm 100:3 WHO and WHAT are we?

_____

Psalm 119:176 HOW have we gone astray?

_____

Throughout the Bible, God and Jesus refer to us as being like sheep. WHAT are sheep like? Do you know? Check out the "inside information" below.

TOP-SECRET FACTS ABOUT SHEEP

Sheep are the dumbest of animals. They are helpless and get scared very easily. They have very little self-defense and will walk right into danger. They won't even try to run to safety. Instead, they will freeze and not even cry out. Sheep also do what all the other sheep are doing. If one gets scared and runs, the others will, too!

Sheep are very stubborn animals. They need a shepherd to guide them. If they are left on their own, they will go the wrong way, eat the wrong food, and drink the wrong water. If a shepherd doesn't lead them to new pastures, they will live in a rut. Sheep will even eat themselves right off a cliff. They will plunge over the edge to injury or death just to get that last mouthful of grass.

Sheep can become cast down. They can get turned over and stuck on their backs and die in a state of panic if the shepherd doesn't turn them right side up right away.

Sheep are bothered by pests. They get flies and gnats up their nose, and these pests lay eggs in there. When the eggs hatch, the growing larvae irritate the sheep's nose. Sheep will beat their heads against trees or rocks to try to get these pests to stop bothering them. The shepherd puts oil on the sheep's head and around its nose to kill these pests.*

So do you see WHY the Lord compares us to sheep? Do we get scared, go the wrong way, give in to peer pressure, and

---

* The information about sheep was gathered from Phillip Keller's book *A Shepherd Looks at Psalm 23*.

do dumb things? Are we stubborn and determined to do it our way? Yes! That's why we need a shepherd.

Go back to page 129 and read Psalm 23 again.

> Psalm 23:1 WHAT happens when the Lord is my Shepherd?
> I shall not _____.

When the Lord is our Shepherd, we will have all that we will ever need. There is no want. As you look at the rest of the verses in Psalm 23, write out WHAT the Lord does.

> Psalm 23:2-6 He makes me _____ _____ in green pastures. He _____ me beside quiet waters, He _____ my soul, He _____ me in the paths of _____. He is _____ me, so there is no reason to fear. His rod and staff _____ me. He _____ a table before me. He _____ my head with oil.

Wow! WHY would we ever choose to go our own way? Our Shepherd has all we will ever need. When we are hungry, scared, lost, and bothered by pests (people who hurt us, bad thoughts) all we have to do is run to the Lord, our Shepherd. He will lead us to quiet waters. He will restore our soul. He is all that we need!

Now practice your memory verse. Tomorrow will find out just how the Lord takes care of our needs!

Day Five

CODE NAME: SHEPHERD

Guess what, GSAs? Today we get to learn how to do coordinated rapid room entries. Doesn't that sound like fun? But first we need to continue gathering the intel on our Shepherd. So don't forget to pray, and then we're good to go!

Turn to your Observation Worksheet on page 189. Read John 10:1-17 and 26-28 and mark the following key words:

Shepherd (draw a brown staff)

sheep

Now gather the intel.

John 10:1 WHO is speaking in this verse? If you don't know, remember context (look at the verses that come before or after John 10:1). Read John 10:7 to discover WHO is speaking.

_____

John 10:11 WHO is Jesus?

_____

Let's make a list about the shepherd.

John 10:2 The shepherd enters by the _____.

John 10:3 The shepherd _____ the sheep, and they _____ his voice. He _____ them out.

John 10:11,15 The good shepherd _____ _____ His _____ for the sheep.

John 10:12 The shepherd is the o __ __ __ r of the sheep.

John 10:14 The good shepherd k __ __ __ s His own.

John 10:27 The sheep f __ __ __ __ w the shepherd.

Isn't that *awesome* to see that Jesus is the good Shepherd who lays down His life for you and me? He is the One who came to seek and save the lost. Read Luke 15:4,5 printed out on the next page.

4 What man among you, if he has a hundred sheep and has lost one of them, does not leave the ninety-nine in the open pasture and go after the one which is lost until he finds it? **5** When he has found it, he lays it on his shoulders, rejoicing.

Luke 15:4 WHAT does the man do if he loses one of his sheep?

_____

Luke 15:5 WHAT does he do when he finds it?

_____

Every single lamb matters to the good Shepherd.

Now go back and read John 10:27,28 again.

John 10:27 WHAT do the sheep do when they hear the shepherd's voice? _____

John 10:28 WHAT does Jesus, the good Shepherd, give the sheep (us)?

_____

Can anyone snatch us out of Jesus' hand? No way! Because Jesus is the Shepherd and the Guardian of our souls, no one can snatch us out of His hands. Not only is Jesus Jehovah-raah, our Shepherd, but He is also Jehovah-jireh. He provided for our salvation. He is the Lamb of God that takes away the sin of the world (John 1:29).

Now that you have seen HOW much Jehovah-raah cares for you, will you let Him be your Shepherd? Will you let Him lead, guide, and protect you? If you do, your cup will overflow. Surely goodness and lovingkindness will follow you all the days of your life, and you will dwell in the house of the Lord forever.

6

OUT IN THE OPEN—GOD'S NAMES REVEALED

Last week as we cracked our secret codes to reveal God's names, we discovered that God is our Peace, our Deliverer, and our Shepherd. Isn't that awesome? We don't have to worry or be afraid because we can rest in Him. He is our Peace. His name is Jehovah-shalom. When we have failed or our enemy comes against us, we know that He will deliver us because He is Jehovah-sabaoth. And He is there to lead and guide us because He is Jehovah-raah, our Shepherd.

Amazing! Now let's head back to the cabin to see what Uncle Matt has in store for us as we crack the rest of God's code names to reveal just *how* awesome our God is.

BREAKING THE CODE

"Hey, guys," Uncle Matt said as he walked outside on the deck to meet Max, Molly, Colby, Ruthi, and Sam. "Did you remember to bring the newspaper today?"

"We sure did," Max replied. "What are we going to do with the newspaper?"

"Well, Max, one of the ways secret agents pass secret messages is through the newspaper. So I want you to see if you can spy out the encoded message in the newspaper that will reveal God's name. Look for the ad for the new paintball store."

As they looked through the newspaper, Colby spotted it first. "Is this it, Uncle Matt?" he laughed. "The ad for Sam's Sporting Goods Store?"

"That's it. Now look at all the numbers used in the ad. That's your secret code. To decode God's name, use the Number Cipher Secret Code below and replace the numbers in the ad with letters by writing the letters out on the lines underneath the ad."

OK, GSAs, decode the newspaper ad below. Start by finding the first number in the ad—number 10. Now what letter in the cipher code replaces 10? J. So write the letter J on the line below. Do this for each number until you have uncovered God's new name.

Grand Opening June 10 for Sam's Sporting Goods. Paintballs on sale $5–$8. Paintball guns 15%–22% off through July 1. 8 new models to choose from arriving on June 20th. Sale price only $19.94. Store hours 11–5 Monday–Saturday. We're located at Plaza 14 on 21st Street.

_____ - _____

NUMBER CIPHER SECRET CODE

A	B	C	D	E	F	G	H	I	J	K	L	M	N
1	2	3	4	5	6	7	8	9	10	11	12	13	14

O	P	Q	R	S	T	U	V	W	X	Y	Z
15	16	17	18	19	20	21	22	23	24	25	26

All right! You are becoming quite a spy! Now let's discover the meaning of this name *Jehovah-tsidkenu* (pronounced *je-HOE-vah sid-KAY-new*) by looking at the first time it is revealed, in Jeremiah 23.

This is a very dark time for the nation of Judah. The whole nation has corrupted themselves. They have sinned big-time, except for a small remnant. It is during this very dark time that God reveals Himself to His people as Jehovah-tsidkenu in order to give them hope for the future.

WHAT does this name mean? Let's find out. Read Jeremiah 23:5,6 printed out below.

> **5** "Behold, the days are coming," declares the
> LORD, "when I will raise up for David a righteous
> Branch; and He will reign as king and act wisely
> and do justice and righteousness in the land. **6** In
> His days Judah will be saved, and Israel will dwell
> securely; and this is His name by which He will be
> called, 'The LORD our righteousness.' "

Jeremiah 23:5 WHO is the Lord going to raise up for David?

_____

WHAT will this righteous branch do?

_____

Jeremiah 23:6 WHAT is the name He will be called?

_____

You have just discovered the meaning of God's name Jehovah-tsidkenu. It means "The Lord Our Righteousness." So WHO is the righteous branch that God is talking about in Jeremiah who will reign as king, act wisely, and do justice and righteousness in the land? WHO is the branch that is called The Lord Our Righteousness?

Use your Operations Manual to look up and read Luke 1:31-33. WHO comes from the throne of David, will be called the Son of the Most High, and will reign over the house of Jacob forever? _____

Jesus! Jesus is the righteous branch of David. He is The Lord Our Righteousness. Do you remember what we learned about being righteous? Being righteous is to be made right with God. HOW can we be made right with God? Do you remember? Is there anything we can do to be made righteous?

Let's find out. Read Romans 3:10,11 printed out below.

> **10** as it is written, "There is none righteous, not even one; **11** there is none who understands, there is none who seeks for God."

Is anyone righteous, according to these verses? _____

Now read Romans 3:22,23 printed out below.

> **22** ...even the righteousness of God through faith in Jesus Christ for all those who believe; for there is no distinction; **23** for all have sinned and fall short of the glory of God.

Romans 3:22 WHERE does the righteousness of God come from?

_____

Romans 3:23 WHO has sinned? _____

Read Romans 9:31,32 printed out below.

> **31** But Israel, pursuing a law of righteousness, did not arrive at that law. **32** Why? Because they did not pursue it by faith, but as though it were by works. They stumbled over the stumbling stone.

Did Israel arrive at righteousness? _____

WHY or WHY not?

_____

HOW did Israel pursue righteousness? By w __ __ __ s

Can we become righteous with the good things we do?
_____

Read Isaiah 64:6 printed out below.

> *For all of us have become like one who is unclean, and all our righteous deeds are like a filthy garment.*

WHAT are our righteous deeds like?

_____

Read Romans 10:9,10 printed out below.

> **9** If you confess with your mouth Jesus as Lord, and believe in your heart that God raised Him from the dead, you will be saved; **10** for with the heart a person believes, resulting in righteousness, and with the mouth he confesses, resulting in salvation.

Romans 10:9 WHAT do you have to do to be saved?

_____

_____

Romans 10:10 When a person believes in his heart and is saved, WHAT is the result?

_____

Read 2 Corinthians 5:20,21 printed out on the next page.

20 Therefore, we are ambassadors for Christ, as though God were making an appeal through us; we beg you on behalf of Christ, be reconciled to God. **21** He made Him who knew no sin to be sin on our behalf, so that we might become the righteousness of God in Him.

2 Corinthians 5:21 WHO was made to be sin on our behalf?

_____

WHY? _____

   Our righteousness is only by faith in Jesus Christ and what He did for us on the cross. It does not come from our works, our good deeds. We can never be good enough, because we are all sinners. The only way we can be made right with a righteous and holy God is through Jesus—the perfect, unblemished Lamb of God, who hung on a cross to be made sin for you and me! Jesus is Jehovah-tsidkenu. He is our righteousness. When God looks at us, He sees Jesus' righteousness instead of our sin. The Lord is our righteousness. All we have to do is trust in His name.
   Now discover your memory verse by using the same Number Cipher Secret Code that you used to decode God's name on page 136.

8-5   13-1-4-5   8-9-13   23-8-15   11-14-5-23   14-15   19-9-14
____   _____   _____   _____   _____   ____   _____

20-15   2-5   19-9-14   15-14   15-21-18   2-5-8-1-12-6,   19-15
_____   ___   _____   ____   _____   _____,   ____

20-8-1-20   23-5   13-9-7-8-20   2-5-3-15-13-5   20-8-5
_____   ____   _____   _____   ____

18-9-7-8-20-5-15-21-19-14-5-19-19   15-6   7-15-4   9-14   8-9-13.
_____   ____   _____   ___   _____

2 Corinthians 5: _____

Great work, GSAs! Now practice it out loud three times today!

RETRIEVING THE MESSAGE

"Well, guys," Uncle Matt said, "we're getting close to the end of our mission. Today as you go out in the open, it's Molly's turn to make contact and retrieve the next secret code that will reveal God's name. Molly, your mission is to go to the park and take a bag of sunflower seeds and your tennis racket. Sit on the bench and feed the birds. Your contact will be a girl in a tennis outfit. She will sit next to you. Ask her if all birds fly south for the winter, and she will respond with, 'All but the cockatoo.' Then she will tell you where to find the next secret code."

OK, GSAs, grab your bikes and head to the park.

As Max, Ruthi, and Colby sat on the park bench behind Molly and listened to her ask the girl if all birds fly south in the winter, they almost cracked up laughing, which made Sam start barking and going crazy. Molly ignored them as the girl responded with "All but the cockatoo" and told Molly, "Tennis is a lot of fun. Why don't you try it?" as she handed Molly a can of tennis balls and got up and walked away.

Molly opened the can of tennis balls as Max, Colby, Ruthi, and Sam rushed over to her park bench. "OK, guys, where do you think the message is hidden?" she asked as she dumped the balls out and peered into the can.

Max thought as he looked over the can. "Let's peel this label off. Maybe it's under there."

Molly very carefully peeled off the label under the lid to discover a piece of paper. "OK, guys, I think this is it. We've done it again. Let's head back to the lake to decode our secret message."

As they all gathered back inside the cabin, Molly asked Uncle Matt, "I think this is another key word code. Am I right?"

"You sure are! Can you figure out what key word was used to make this code?"

Ruthi spoke up first. "Tennis," she guessed.

"That's it!" Uncle Matt replied. "You guys have it down. So get to work and discover God's name."

OK, GSAs, the Key Word Secret Code is below. Here's Molly's message. Now discover God's name.

FSCLVTC-QCTJJTC

_____ - _____

KEY WORD SECRET CODE

T	E	N	I	S	A	B	C	D	F	G	H	J	K
A	B	C	D	E	F	G	H	I	J	K	L	M	N

L	M	O	P	Q	R	U	V	W	X	Y	Z
O	P	Q	R	S	T	U	V	W	X	Y	Z

All right, you did it! You have decoded another of God's names. God's name is *Jehovah-shammah* (pronounced *je-HOE-vah SHAH-mah*). Let's uncover what this name means.

The children of Israel are now in captivity and will be there for 70 years. God has allowed Jerusalem to be conquered by the enemy because of Israel's stubborn disobedience and rejection. God had to judge His people for their sin.

However, God has a promise for them for the future, and it is a promise that has not yet been fulfilled. It is a promise that deals with Jerusalem, the city that the Babylonians destroyed. Let's take a look at this promise in Ezekiel 48:35 printed out below to uncover the meaning of God's name Jehovah-shammah.

> *The city shall be 18,000 cubits round about; and the name of the city from that day shall be, "The LORD is there."*

WHAT is the name of the city?

_____

This is the meaning of God's name Jehovah-shammah: "The Lord is there." God had always been with the children of Israel ever since they had come out of captivity in Egypt. But now because of their sin and disobedience, God is going to leave the city of Jerusalem. The people are devastated. They cannot believe that God would let Jerusalem be destroyed. At the end of Ezekiel in the very last verse, we see God giving His people a message of encouragement to let them know that one day He will return to the city. He does this by telling them that the name of the city is Jehovah-shammah, "The LORD is there."

Isn't it awesome to know that God's name Jehovah-shammah means that He is there? Now let's gather some intel. Let's take a look at some passages of Scripture that show us God's presence in the lives of the children of Israel. Read Exodus 13:20-22 printed out below.

> **20** Then they set out from Succoth and camped in Etham on the edge of the wilderness. **21** The LORD was going before them in a pillar of cloud by day to lead them on the way, and in a pillar of fire by night to give them light, that they might travel by day and by night. **22** He did not take away the pillar of cloud by day, nor the pillar of fire by night, from before the people.

Exodus 13:21 HOW was the Lord with them?

_____

Read Joshua 1:1,2,5 printed out below.

> **1** Now it came about after the death of Moses the servant of the LORD, that the LORD spoke to Joshua the son of Nun, Moses' servant, saying, **2** "Moses My servant is dead; now therefore arise, cross this Jordan, you and all this people, to the land which I am giving to them, to the sons of Israel.... **5** No man will be able to stand before you all the days of your life. Just as I have been with Moses, I will be with you; I will not fail you or forsake you."

Joshua 1:5 WHAT does God tell Joshua after Moses has died?

"I will be _____ _____; I will not _____

you or _____ you."

Read 1 Samuel 4:6,7 printed out below.

> **6** When the Philistines heard the noise of the shout, they said, "What does the noise of this great shout in the camp of the Hebrews mean?" Then they understood that the ark of the LORD had come into the camp. **7** The Philistines were afraid, for they said, "God has come into the camp." And they said, "Woe to us! For nothing like this has happened before."

WHY were the Philistines afraid? WHAT did they realize when the ark of the Lord came into the camp?

_____

Read 2 Chronicles 7:1-3 printed out below.

> **1** Now when Solomon had finished praying, fire came down from heaven and consumed the burnt offering and the sacrifices, and the glory of the

Lord filled the house. **2** The priests could not enter into the house of the Lord because the glory of the Lord filled the Lord's house. **3** All the sons of Israel, seeing the fire come down and the glory of the Lord upon the house, bowed down on the pavement with their faces to the ground, and they worshiped and gave praise to the Lord, saying, "Truly He is good, truly His lovingkindness is everlasting."

WHAT came down from heaven?

_____

WHAT filled the Lord's house?

_____

Did you see in these passages of Scripture how God was always with them? These scriptures bring us from the time the children of Israel left Egypt until the time of Jeremiah and Ezekiel, before God allows them to be taken into captivity. Tomorrow we will take a look at the scriptures that show us HOW God left Jerusalem when He allowed them to be taken into captivity.

Before we head out, ask yourself, "Do I know that God is there? Do I recognize His presence?" He is with you wherever you are and whatever you do. When things are hard and difficult, you need to remember that God is with you. Just call on Him by name!

Action and Adventure

OK, GSAs, are you ready for an action-packed day? Uncle Matt is going to run us through the obstacle course. Then we will practice our bootleg turns in our go-carts. After that Mr. Tim will give us our martial arts lesson. But before the action begins, we need to spend some time gathering our intel so that we are ready to go out in the field when our mission is complete. So spend some time with your Commander in Chief in prayer, and then we're good to go.

Yesterday we revealed that God's name is Jehovah-shammah, "The LORD is there." We also looked at scriptures that showed us God's presence in the lives of the children of Israel from the time they left Egypt up until the time of Jeremiah and Ezekiel, before they were taken into captivity for their sin and disobedience.

Today we are going to take a look at some passages in Ezekiel that show us WHAT happened that caused God so much grief and HOW God left the temple and then the city.

Let's read Ezekiel 8:3-6,17,18 printed out below.

> 3 He stretched out the form of a hand and caught me by a lock of my head; and the Spirit lifted me up between earth and heaven and brought me in the visions of God to Jerusalem, to the entrance of the north gate of the inner court, where the seat of the idol of jealousy, which provokes to jealousy, was located. 4 And behold, the glory of the God of Israel was there, like the appearance which I saw in the plain. 5 Then He said to me, "Son of man, raise your eyes now toward the north." So I raised my eyes toward the north, and behold, to the north of the altar gate was this idol of jealousy at the entrance. 6 And He said to me, "Son of man, do you see what they are doing, the great abominations which the house of Israel are committing here, so that I would be far from My sanctuary? But yet you will see still greater abominations."... 17 He said to me, "Do you see this, son of man? Is it too light a thing for the house of Judah to commit the abominations which they have committed here,

that they have filled the land with violence and
provoked Me repeatedly? For behold, they are putting the twig to their nose. **18** Therefore, I indeed
will deal in wrath. My eye will have no pity nor
will I spare; and though they cry in My ears with a
loud voice, yet I will not listen to them."

Ezekiel 8:4 WHAT was in the temple?

_____

Ezekiel 8:5 WHAT did Ezekiel see as he raised his eyes
toward north of the altar gate?

_____

Ezekiel 8:17 WHAT was the house of Judah committing
in the temple? _____

Do you see WHY God was so grieved? Israel had brought
an idol into God's temple. Can you believe it? No wonder
God was so upset that He allowed them to be taken into captivity.
    Now let's find out HOW God departed the temple by read-
ing the passages of Scripture below.
    Read Ezekiel 10:3,4 printed out below.

3 Now the cherubim were standing on the right
side of the temple when the man entered, and the
cloud filled the inner court. **4** Then the glory of the
LORD went up from the cherub to the threshold of
the temple, and the temple was filled with the
cloud and the court was filled with the brightness
of the glory of the LORD.

Ezekiel 10:4 WHERE did the glory of the Lord go up
from the cherub? _____

Read Ezekiel 10:18 printed out below.

> Then the glory of the LORD departed from the threshold
> of the temple and stood over the cherubim.

WHERE did the glory of the Lord go next?

_____

Read Ezekiel 10:19 printed out below.

> When the cherubim departed, they lifted their wings
> and rose up from the earth in my sight with the wheels
> beside them; and they stood still at the entrance of the
> east gate of the LORD's house, and the glory of the God
> of Israel hovered over them.

WHERE did the cherubim stand after departing?

_____

WHERE was God's glory?

_____

Read Ezekiel 11:22,23 printed out below.

> **22** Then the cherubim lifted up their wings with
> the wheels beside them, and the glory of the God
> of Israel hovered over them. **23** The glory of the
> LORD went up from the midst of the city and stood
> over the mountain which is east of the city.

WHERE did the glory of the Lord go?

_____

Did you notice how God didn't just leave His temple? He
slowly moved from one place to the other, waiting for Israel to

repent, to confess what they had done wrong. God did not want to leave His city. He did it to judge their sin and disobedience. But even though God leaves Jerusalem, He has to come back because He is a covenant-keeping God. He promised them that He is their God and they are His people. He will not leave them forever because God does not break His promises! Now you know why at the end of Ezekiel in Ezekiel 48:35 God tells them that the name of the city will be "The LORD is there." He is encouraging them in their captivity that Jehovah-shammah will return to His city.

WHAT do we see about God's character as we see His anger at the idol being in His temple? Do you know? Guess what? You will find out tomorrow as we discover another one of God's names.

So go outside and get started on your obstacle course training. And while you're at it, work on this week's memory verse!

GUARDING OUR LOYALTY

"I've got it!" Ruthi shouted as she rode her bike into the yard.

"This time the message was in my shoe. How does your Uncle Matt do all these things?"

"Hey, he's just a great secret agent," Max answered. "It sure has been fun having him for the summer. We had better head back to the cabin so we can decode this last name for God. I can't believe our spy adventure is almost over. This has been so much fun!"

Now that everyone is back at the cabin, GSAs, we need to decode the last secret message on the next page by coloring the spaces that have a dot in them red and writing the code word on the line underneath the puzzle.

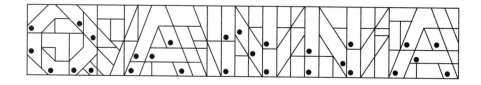

Way to go! Another name of God is revealed. God's name is *Qanna* (pronounced *ka-NAH*). WHAT does this name mean? Let's find out. Read Exodus 20:1-6 printed out below.

1 Then God spoke all these words, saying, **2** "I am the LORD your God, who brought you out of the land of Egypt, out of the house of slavery. **3** You shall have no other gods before Me. **4** You shall not make for yourself an idol, or any likeness of what is in heaven above or on the earth beneath or in the water under the earth. **5** You shall not worship them or serve them; for I, the LORD your God, am a jealous God, visiting the iniquity of the fathers on the children, on the third and the fourth generations of those who hate Me, **6** but showing lovingkindness to thousands, to those who love Me and keep My commandments."

Exodus 20:3 WHAT does God tell the children of Israel?

_____

Did they have any other gods (idols) before their God in the temple in Ezekiel 8? _____

Exodus 20:5 WHAT does God say about Himself?

_____

Now read Exodus 34:12-14 printed out below.

> **12** Watch yourself that you make no covenant with the inhabitants of the land into which you are going, or it will become a snare in your midst. **13** But rather, you are to tear down their altars and smash their sacred pillars and cut down their Asherim **14** —for you shall not worship any other god, for the LORD, whose name is Jealous, is a jealous God.

Exodus 34:14 WHAT is God's name?

_____

This is the meaning of God's name Qanna. God is a jealous God. The children of Israel could not believe that God would let Israel fall, yet they forgot God's name. They put other gods before the one true God.

Now read 2 Corinthians 11:2 printed out below.

> *For I am jealous for you with a godly jealousy; for I betrothed you to one husband, so that to Christ I might present you as a pure virgin.*

WHAT kind of jealousy does God have?

_____

God is a holy and righteous God. He acted according to His name Qanna. Now ask yourself: "Have I put anything in God's place? Are there any idols in my life?" An idol is anything that keeps you from following God fully—it keeps you away from God, instead of drawing you to God.

Ask yourself: "Do I care more about my friends and the crowd's approval than I do about God? Is what I wear more important than who I am? Do I have time to watch TV and play sports and video games, but have no time to read the

Bible and pray?" Examine your heart to see WHAT is first in your life. Write it out below.

_____

Now let's go back to God's name Jehovah-shammah, The Lord is there. Do we ever see God come back to His temple? Let's find out. Read John 1:1,14 printed out below.

> **1** In the beginning was the Word, and the Word was with God, and the Word was God.... **14** And the Word became flesh, and dwelt among us, and we saw His glory, glory as of the only begotten from the Father, full of grace and truth.

WHO was the Word?

The Word was _____.

The Word was with _____. WHO is this? WHO

became flesh and dwelt among them? _____

Is Jesus God? _____

Did they see His glory? _____

Now read Luke 2:27-32 printed out below. This is when Jesus was brought as an infant to be presented to the Lord.

> **27** And [Simeon] came in the Spirit into the temple; and when the parents brought in the child Jesus, to carry out for Him the custom of the Law, **28** then he took Him into his arms, and blessed God, and said, **29** "Now Lord, You are releasing Your bond-servant to depart in peace, according to Your word; **30** for my eyes have seen Your salvation, **31** which You have prepared in the presence of all peoples, **32** a Light of revelation to the Gentiles, and the glory of Your people Israel."

WHERE did Jesus' parents bring Jesus?

_____

So did God return to the temple? Yes, He did as Jesus. Remember, Jesus is God. So when Jesus was brought into the temple by His earthly parents, God was there. However, most of Israel did not believe that Jesus was God (John 1:11,12). And as an adult, Jesus, the mighty God, came to Jerusalem and entered her gates, taught in her temple, healed the sick, held the children, fed the people, and wept with them. God lived in their very presence. But they rejected Him, and in the end He died for them. WHAT happened after Jesus died and was resurrected? He left to go and be with His Father, but He did not leave us alone. He left us a Helper, the Holy Spirit.

Read John 14:23-26 printed out below.

> **23** Jesus answered and said to him, "If anyone loves Me, he will keep My word; and My Father will love him, and We will come to him and make Our abode with him. **24** He who does not love Me does not keep My words; and the word which you hear is not Mine, but the Father's who sent Me. **25** These things I have spoken to you while abiding with you. **26** But the Helper, the Holy Spirit, whom the Father will send in My name, He will teach you all things, and bring to your remembrance all that I said to you."

John 14:23 WHAT does God—the Father, Jesus, and the Holy Spirit—do if we love Him and keep His word?

_____

Isn't that awesome? God is Jehovah-shammah, He is there. When we believe in Jesus and are saved, the Holy Spirit comes to live inside us. We are never alone or forsaken because God is there! God's presence is with us because He lives inside us!

Now read God's promise in Revelation 21:1-5 printed out on the next page.

1 Then I saw a new heaven and a new earth; for the first heaven and the first earth passed away, and there is no longer any sea. **2** And I saw the holy city, new Jerusalem, coming down out of heaven from God, made ready as a bride adorned for her husband. **3** And I heard a loud voice from the throne, saying, "Behold, the tabernacle of God is among men, and He will dwell among them, and they shall be His people, and God Himself will be among them, **4** and He will wipe away every tear from their eyes; and there will no longer be any death; there will no longer be any mourning, or crying, or pain; the first things have passed away." **5** And He who sits on the throne said, "Behold, I am making all things new." And He said, "Write, for these words are faithful and true."

Revelation 21:3 WHAT will the tabernacle of God do?

God came as the Lord Jesus Christ. He is here now as the Holy Spirit, and one day He will come again as the King of kings to rule over all the nations of the earth. God promised that He would return to Jerusalem, and the name of Jerusalem would be Jehovah-shammah. When He returns, what He promised through Ezekiel will be fulfilled. One day Jehovah-shammah will make His permanent dwelling among men. Just remember when you feel lost or forsaken that you are not alone. God is Jehovah-shammah. He is there! If you have believed in the Lord Jesus Christ, then He lives inside you!

THE FINAL OPERATION

Well, GSAs, this is our last day at Uncle Matt's cabin. Today Uncle Matt is going to test our secret agent skills to see if we are ready to work officially as God's secret agents. Are you ready to go out on the mission field (your school and neighborhood) and share with other people what we have discovered about God and Jesus? Are you ready to work officially as a secret agent for God?

Then let's get started on our final operation. You have uncovered all of God's names, but your mission isn't quite complete. You need to work on knowing these names because Psalm 9:10 tells us,

> And those who know Your name will put their trust in You, for You, O LORD, have not forsaken those who seek You.

God will never forsake you if you seek Him, if you know His name and put your trust in Him. That's why this is such an important mission. HOW can you become God's secret agents if you don't know Him by name?

So today we're going to put all the intel that we have gathered into action by first reviewing the last nine names of God that we have discovered. Draw a picture in each box on the next two pages to help you remember each one of these nine names of God you have discovered. Then write out what the name means. Under the name Jehovah-rapha write out The Lord Who Heals. Then draw a picture or a symbol to remind you that the Lord is your Healer. Do this for each name of God. Use your imagination and have fun!

Jehovah-rapha
The Lord _____

Jehovah-nissi
The Lord is my _____

Jehovah-mekoddishkem
The Lord who _____

Jehovah-shalom
The Lord is _____

Jehovah-sabaoth
The Lord of _____

Jehovah-raah
The Lord is my _____

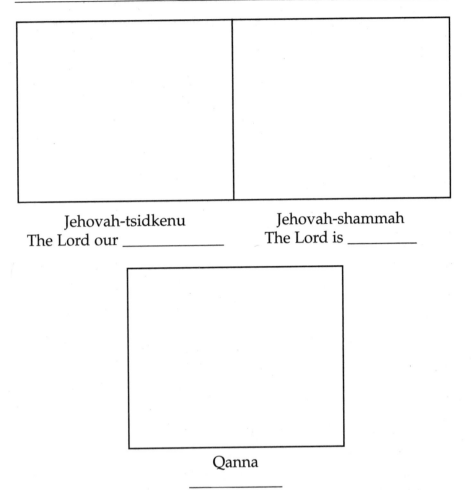

Jehovah-tsidkenu
The Lord our _____

Jehovah-shammah
The Lord is _____

Qanna
_____

Way to go! Now let's put it all together before you head out into the field for one more paintball battle. Uncle Matt is ready to put you to the test. Use those great memorization skills to help you earn your secret agent badge of service. Below are all of the 16 Hebrew names of God that we have revealed. Match each name with its meaning. See if you can do it from memory without looking back in your book.

____ Elohim   A. The Lord Is Peace

____ El Elyon   B. The Lord Our
                                        Righteousness

____ El Roi   C. The Lord Who Sanctifies

____ El Shaddai   D. The Lord Is Our Healer

____ Adonai   E. The Lord of hosts—God
                                        is our Deliverer

____ Jehovah   F. The Lord is there

____ Jehovah-jireh   G. The Creator

____ Jehovah-rapha   H. The Lord is my Shepherd

____ Jehovah-nissi   I. Jealous

____ Jehovah-mekoddishkem   J. LORD, the self-existent
                                        One

____ Jehovah-shalom   K. God Most High—God is
                                        sovereign

____ Jehovah-sabaoth   L. The Lord Will Provide

____ Jehovah-raah   M. Lord, Master

____ Jehovah-tsidkenu   N. Almighty God—the all-
                                        sufficient One

____ Jehovah-shammah   O. The Lord Is My Banner

____ Qanna   P. God sees

MISSION ACCOMPLISHED!

All right! Way to go! You did it! You have earned your secret agent badge of service. We are so proud of you!

Just look at all you have learned. You know all about spying out truth. You have learned how to mark key words, make lists, gather hidden intel by asking the 5 W's and an H, and how to decode and encode secret messages.

But most importantly, you know your God. You have revealed His names. You have learned that God is the Creator. He created you by weaving you in your mother's womb. You are fearfully and wonderfully made! You also know that God is God Most High, the sovereign Ruler over all the earth. You know that God sees everything, that He is sufficient for all your needs, and that He is your Lord and Master. Have you surrendered your life to the Lord Jesus Christ?

God is also Jehovah, the self-existent One who is the I AM. He is Jehovah-jireh, your Provider. He has given you eternal life by sacrificing His very own Son, and through Him He will provide everything that you need (Philippians 4:19). Look at how much He loves you! God is also your Healer, your Banner, and He is the One who sanctifies you, who sets you apart. God is your Peace, Deliverer, and Shepherd. Will you let Him lead and guide your life?

You have discovered that God is a jealous God, that we are not to put anyone or anything before Him. We are to love Him with all our heart, soul, and mind. We are not to have any idols in our lives. You saw that the Lord is your Righteousness, and that His name is Jehovah-shammah—He is there. One day very soon He will come back for you and me! That is going to be one very exciting adventure!

Don't forget to fill out the card in the back of this book. We have a special certificate that we want to send you for spying out truth and becoming one of God's secret agents.

We hate for this adventure to come to an end, but God is ready to put you into active service. You have done an *awesome* job! Now that you have learned to spy out truth, it's up to you. Will you take what you have learned and let God change and transform your life?

Now go out in the open and recruit other kids as you live a life of service to our King. See you for another adventure in God's Word real soon!

Molly, Max, and

Guess Who?

P.S. Now, that you know God's names, you might like to make some banners for your room. Here's how you can do it.

First you will need fabric for your banner. If you want to appliqué on your banner, you will also need different fabrics for your appliqué design. You can use felt, cotton, or any other fabric.

You will also need a pen, scissors, fabric glue, and a wooden dowel to hang your banner. To decorate your banner you can use fabric paint, trims, buttons, beads, sequins, yarn, fringe, or whatever you choose.

To make your banner, cut your fabric to the size and shape that you want. Then if you want to appliqué on your banner, you can draw or trace your design, letters, or symbol on the fabric you have chosen for your appliqué. Cut out your design and use fabric glue to apply it to your banner.

If you don't want to do an appliqué, you can make your banner by simply using fabric paint, glue, and glitter to draw and paint your design on your banner. You can also use fringe for decoration around the outside edges of your banner.

To hang your banner, wrap the top of your fabric around a wooden dowel and glue it or staple it to the banner. Use your imagination and have fun!

PUZZLE ANSWERS

Page 10

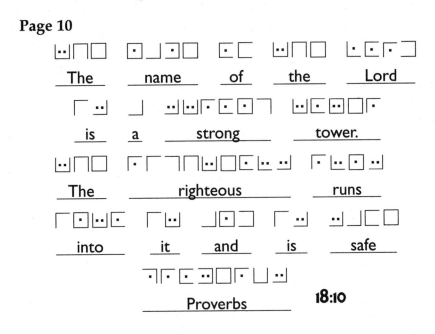

The name of the Lord

is a strong tower.

The righteous runs

into it and is safe

Proverbs 18:10

Page 44

I will cry to God Most High, to God who accomplishes all things for me.

—Psalm 57:2

Page 47

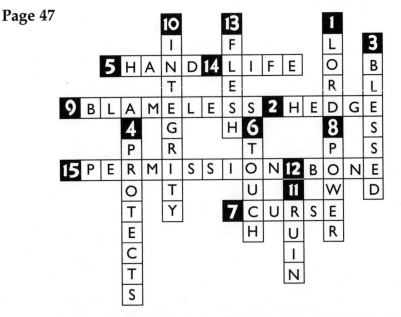

Page 54

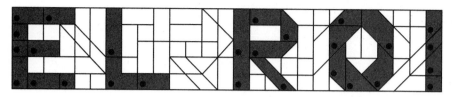

Page 74

E SPER TK TDN HKQR, "YKU PQN IY
I SAID TO THE LORD YOU ARE MY

HKQR; E DPVN JK BKKR ONSERNS YKU."
LORD I HAVE NO GOOD BESIDES YOU

LSPHI 16:2
PSALM

Page 81

J E H O V A H

J I R E H

Page 83

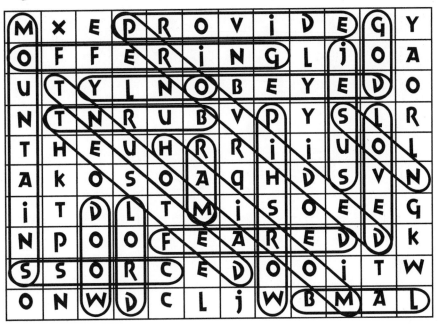

Page 94

PVJF GV, K FKNO, JIO B WBFF EV
HEAL ME O LORD AND I WILL BE

PVJFVO; QJUV GV JIO B WBFF EV
HEALED SAVE ME AND I WILL BE

QJUVO, AKN YKT JNV GY LNJBQV.
SAVED FOR YOU ARE MY PRAISE

CVNVGBJP 17:14
JEREMIAH

Page 116

Page 119

KVZXV   R   OVZEV   DRGS   BLF;   NB   KVZXV
<u>PEACE</u>   <u>I</u>   <u>LEAVE</u>   <u>WITH</u>   <u>YOU</u>   <u>MY</u>   <u>PEACE</u>

R   TREV   GL   BLF;   MLG   ZH   GSV   DLIOW
<u>I</u>   <u>GIVE</u>   <u>TO</u>   <u>YOU</u>   <u>NOT</u>   <u>AS</u>   <u>THE</u>   <u>WORLD</u>

TREVH   WL   R   TREV   GL   BLF.   WL   MLG
<u>GIVES</u>   <u>DO</u>   <u>I</u>   <u>GIVE</u>   <u>TO</u>   <u>YOU</u>   <u>DO</u>   <u>NOT</u>

OVG   BLFI   SVZIG   YV   GILFYOVW,   MLI   OVG
<u>LET</u>   <u>YOUR</u>   <u>HEART</u>   <u>BE</u>   <u>TROUBLED</u>   <u>NOR</u>   <u>LET</u>

RG   YV   UVZIUFO.
<u>IT</u>   <u>BE</u>   <u>FEARFUL</u>

QLSM 14:27
<u>JOHN</u>

Page 140

8-5	13-1-4-5	8-9-13	23-8-15	11-14-5-23	14-15	19-9-14
HE	MADE	HIM	WHO	KNEW	NO	SIN

20-15	2-5	19-9-14	15-14	15-21-18	2-5-8-1-12-6,	19-15
TO	BE	SIN	ON	OUR	BEHALF	SO

20-8-1-20	23-5	13-9-7-8-20	2-5-3-15-13-5	20-8-5
THAT	WE	MIGHT	BECOME	THE

18-9-7-8-20-5-15-21-19-14-5-19-19	15-6	7-15-4	9-14	8-9-13
RIGHTEOUSNESS	OF	GOD	IN	HIM

2 Corinthians 5: __21__

Page 150

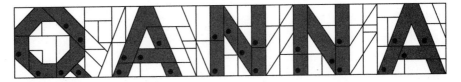

Pages 157–58

G—Elohim, K—El Elyon, P—El Roi, N—El Shaddai,
M—Adonai, J—Jehovah, L—Jehovah-jireh, D—Jehovah-rapha,
O—Jehovah-nissi, C—Jehovah-mekoddishkem,
A—Jehovah-shalom, E—Jehovah-sabaoth, H—Jehovah-raah,
B—Jehovah-tsidkenu, F—Jehovah-shammah, I-Qanna

OBSERVATION WORKSHEETS

PSALM 139

1   O LORD, You have searched me and known *me*.

2   You know when I sit down and when I rise up;
You understand my thought from afar.

3   You scrutinize my path and my lying down,
And are intimately acquainted with all my ways.

4   Even before there is a word on my tongue,
Behold, O LORD, You know it all.

5   You have enclosed me behind and before,
And laid Your hand upon me.

6   *Such* knowledge is too wonderful for me;
It is *too* high, I cannot attain to it.

7   Where can I go from Your Spirit?
Or where can I flee from Your presence?

8   If I ascend to heaven, You are there;
If I make my bed in Sheol, behold, You are there.

9   If I take the wings of the dawn,
If I dwell in the remotest part of the sea,

10   Even there Your hand will lead me,
And Your right hand will lay hold of me.

11   If I say, "Surely the darkness will overwhelm me,
And the light around me will be night,"

12   Even the darkness is not dark to You,
And the night is as bright as the day.
Darkness and light are alike *to You*.

13   For You formed my inward parts;
You wove me in my mother's womb.

14   I will give thanks to You, for I am fearfully and wonderfully made;

Wonderful are Your works,

And my soul knows it very well.

15   My frame was not hidden from You,

When I was made in secret,

And skillfully wrought in the depths of the earth;

16   Your eyes have seen my unformed substance;

And in Your book were all written

The days that were ordained *for me,*

When as yet there was not one of them.

17   How precious also are Your thoughts to me, O God!

How vast is the sum of them!

18   If I should count them, they would outnumber the sand.

When I awake, I am still with You.

19   O that You would slay the wicked, O God;

Depart from me, therefore, men of bloodshed.

20   For they speak against You wickedly,

And Your enemies take *Your name* in vain.

21   Do I not hate those who hate You, O Lord?

And do I not loathe those who rise up against You?

22   I hate them with the utmost hatred;

They have become my enemies.

23   Search me, O God, and know my heart;

Try me and know my anxious thoughts;

24   And see if there be any hurtful way in me,

And lead me in the everlasting way.

isaiah 43

1   But now, thus says the Lord, your Creator, O Jacob,

And He who formed you, O Israel,

"Do not fear, for I have redeemed you;

I have called you by name; you are Mine!

2   "When you pass through the waters, I will be with you;

And through the rivers, they will not overflow you.

When you walk through the fire, you will not be scorched,

Nor will the flame burn you.

3   "For I am the LORD your God,

The Holy One of Israel, your Savior;

I have given Egypt as your ransom,

Cush and Seba in your place.

4   "Since you are precious in My sight,

Since you are honored and I love you,

I will give *other* men in your place and *other* peoples in exchange for your life.

5   "Do not fear, for I am with you;

I will bring your offspring from the east,

And gather you from the west.

6   "I will say to the north, 'Give *them* up!'

And to the south, 'Do not hold *them* back.'

Bring My sons from afar

And My daughters from the ends of the earth,

7   Everyone who is called by My name,

And whom I have created for My glory,

Whom I have formed, even whom I have made."

8   Bring out the people who are blind, even though they have eyes,

And the deaf, even though they have ears.

9   All the nations have gathered together

So that the peoples may be assembled.

Who among them can declare this

And proclaim to us the former things?

Let them present their witnesses that they may be justified,

Or let them hear and say, "It is true."

10   "You are My witnesses," declares the LORD,

"And My servant whom I have chosen,

So that you may know and believe Me

And understand that I am He.

Before Me there was no God formed,

And there will be none after Me.

11   "I, even I, am the LORD,

And there is no savior besides Me.

12   "It is I who have declared and saved and proclaimed,

And there was no strange *god* among you;

So you are My witnesses," declares the LORD,

"And I am God.

13   "Even from eternity I am He,

And there is none who can deliver out of My hand;

I act and who can reverse it?"

14   Thus says the LORD your Redeemer, the Holy One of Israel,

"For your sake I have sent to Babylon,

And will bring them all down as fugitives,

Even the Chaldeans, into the ships in which they rejoice.

15   "I am the LORD, your Holy One,

The Creator of Israel, your King."

16   Thus says the LORD,

Who makes a way through the sea

And a path through the mighty waters,

17   Who brings forth the chariot and the horse,

The army and the mighty man

(They will lie down together *and* not rise again;

They have been quenched *and* extinguished like a wick):

18 "Do not call to mind the former things,

Or ponder things of the past.

19 "Behold, I will do something new,

Now it will spring forth;

Will you not be aware of it?

I will even make a roadway in the wilderness,

Rivers in the desert.

20 "The beasts of the field will glorify Me,

The jackals and the ostriches,

Because I have given waters in the wilderness

And rivers in the desert,

To give drink to My chosen people.

21 "The people whom I formed for Myself

Will declare My praise.

22 "Yet you have not called on Me, O Jacob;

But you have become weary of Me, O Israel.

23 "You have not brought to Me the sheep of your

burnt offerings,

Nor have you honored Me with your sacrifices.

I have not burdened you with offerings,

Nor wearied you with incense.

24 "You have bought Me not sweet cane with money,

Nor have you filled Me with the fat of your sacrifices;

Rather you have burdened Me with your sins,

You have wearied Me with your iniquities.

25 "I, even I, am the one who wipes out your transgressions for My

own sake,

And I will not remember your sins.

26 "Put Me in remembrance, let us argue our case together;

State your *cause,* that you may be proved right.

27 "Your first forefather sinned,

And your spokesmen have transgressed against Me.

28 "So I will pollute the princes of the sanctuary,

And I will consign Jacob to the ban and Israel to revilement.

Daniel 4

1 Nebuchadnezzar the king to all the peoples, nations, and *men of every* language that live in all the earth: "May your peace abound!

2 "It has seemed good to me to declare the signs and wonders which the Most High God has done for me.

3 "How great are His signs

And how mighty are His wonders!

His kingdom is an everlasting kingdom

And His dominion is from generation to generation.

4 "I, Nebuchadnezzar, was at ease in my house and flourishing in my palace.

5 "I saw a dream and it made me fearful; and *these* fantasies *as I lay* on my bed and the visions in my mind kept alarming me.

6 "So I gave orders to bring into my presence all the wise men of Babylon, that they might make known to me the interpretation of the dream.

7 "Then the magicians, the conjurers, the Chaldeans and the diviners came in and I related the dream to them, but they could not make its interpretation known to me.

8 "But finally Daniel came in before me, whose name is Belteshazzar according to the name of my god, and in whom is a spirit of the holy gods; and I related the dream to him, *saying,*

9 'O Belteshazzar, chief of the magicians, since I know that a spirit of the holy gods is in you and no mystery baffles you, tell *me* the visions of my dream which I have seen, along with its interpretation.

10   'Now *these were* the visions in my mind *as I lay* on my bed: I was looking, and behold, *there was* a tree in the midst of the earth and its height *was* great.

11   'The tree grew large and became strong

And its height reached to the sky,

And it *was* visible to the end of the whole earth.

12   'Its foliage *was* beautiful and its fruit abundant,

And in it *was* food for all.

The beasts of the field found shade under it,

And the birds of the sky dwelt in its branches,

And all living creatures fed themselves from it.

13   'I was looking in the visions in my mind *as I lay* on my bed, and behold, an *angelic* watcher, a holy one, descended from heaven.

14   'He shouted out and spoke as follows:

"Chop down the tree and cut off its branches,

Strip off its foliage and scatter its fruit;

Let the beasts flee from under it

And the birds from its branches.

15   "Yet leave the stump with its roots in the ground,

But with a band of iron and bronze *around it*

In the new grass of the field;

And let him be drenched with the dew of heaven,

And let him share with the beasts in the grass of the earth.

16   "Let his mind be changed from *that of* a man

And let a beast's mind be given to him,

And let seven periods of time pass over him.

17   "This sentence is by the decree of the *angelic* watchers

And the decision is a command of the holy ones,

In order that the living may know

That the Most High is ruler over the realm of mankind,

And bestows it on whom He wishes

And sets over it the lowliest of men."

18 'This is the dream *which* I, King Nebuchadnezzar, have seen. Now you, Belteshazzar, tell *me* its interpretation, inasmuch as none of the wise men of my kingdom is able to make known to me the interpretation; but you are able, for a spirit of the holy gods is in you.'

19 "Then Daniel, whose name is Belteshazzar, was appalled for a while as his thoughts alarmed him. The king responded and said, 'Belteshazzar, do not let the dream or its interpretation alarm you.' Belteshazzar replied, 'My lord, *if only* the dream applied to those who hate you and its interpretation to your adversaries!

20 'The tree that you saw, which became large and grew strong, whose height reached to the sky and was visible to all the earth

21 and whose foliage *was* beautiful and its fruit abundant, and in which *was* food for all, under which the beasts of the field dwelt and in whose branches the birds of the sky lodged—

22 it is you, O king; for you have become great and grown strong, and your majesty has become great and reached to the sky and your dominion to the end of the earth.

23 'In that the king saw an *angelic* watcher, a holy one, descending from heaven and saying, "Chop down the tree and destroy it; yet leave the stump with its roots in the ground, but with a band of iron and bronze *around it* in the new grass of the field, and let him be drenched with the dew of heaven, and let him share with the beasts of the field until seven periods of time pass over him,"

24 this is the interpretation, O king, and this is the decree of the Most High, which has come upon my lord the king:

25 that you be driven away from mankind and your dwelling place be with the beasts of the field, and you be given grass to eat like cattle and be drenched with the dew of heaven; and seven periods of time will pass

over you, until you recognize that the Most High is ruler over the realm of mankind and bestows it on whomever He wishes.

26   'And in that it was commanded to leave the stump with the roots of the tree, your kingdom will be assured to you after you recognize that *it is* Heaven *that* rules.

27   'Therefore, O king, may my advice be pleasing to you: break away now from your sins by *doing* righteousness and from your iniquities by showing mercy to *the* poor, in case there may be a prolonging of your prosperity.'

28   "All *this* happened to Nebuchadnezzar the king.

29   "Twelve months later he was walking on the *roof of* the royal palace of Babylon.

30   "The king reflected and said, 'Is this not Babylon the great, which I myself have built as a royal residence by the might of my power and for the glory of my majesty?'

31   "While the word *was* in the king's mouth, a voice came from heaven, *saying,* 'King Nebuchadnezzar, to you it is declared: sovereignty has been removed from you,

32   and you will be driven away from mankind, and your dwelling place *will be* with the beasts of the field. You will be given grass to eat like cattle, and seven periods of time will pass over you until you recognize that the Most High is ruler over the realm of mankind and bestows it on whomever He wishes.'

33   "Immediately the word concerning Nebuchadnezzar was fulfilled; and he was driven away from mankind and began eating grass like cattle, and his body was drenched with the dew of heaven until his hair had grown like eagles' *feathers* and his nails like birds' *claws.*

34   "But at the end of that period, I, Nebuchadnezzar, raised my eyes toward heaven and my reason returned to me, and I blessed the Most High and praised and honored Him who lives forever;

For His dominion is an everlasting dominion,

And His kingdom *endures* from generation to generation.

35   "All the inhabitants of the earth are accounted as nothing,

But He does according to His will in the host of heaven

And *among* the inhabitants of earth;

And no one can ward off His hand

Or say to Him, 'What have You done?'

36   "At that time my reason returned to me. And my majesty and splendor were restored to me for the glory of my kingdom, and my counselors and my nobles began seeking me out; so I was reestablished in my sovereignty, and surpassing greatness was added to me.

37   "Now I, Nebuchadnezzar, praise, exalt and honor the King of heaven, for all His works are true and His ways just, and He is able to humble those who walk in pride."

JOB 1

1   There was a man in the land of Uz whose name was Job; and that man was blameless, upright, fearing God and turning away from evil.

2   Seven sons and three daughters were born to him.

3   His possessions also were 7,000 sheep, 3,000 camels, 500 yoke of oxen, 500 female donkeys, and very many servants; and that man was the greatest of all the men of the east.

4   His sons used to go and hold a feast in the house of each one on his day, and they would send and invite their three sisters to eat and drink with them.

5   When the days of feasting had completed their cycle, Job would send and consecrate them, rising up early in the morning and offering burnt offerings *according to* the number of them all; for Job said, "Perhaps my sons have sinned and cursed God in their hearts." Thus Job did continually.

6   Now there was a day when the sons of God came to present themselves before the LORD, and Satan also came among them.

7   The LORD said to Satan, "From where do you come?" Then Satan
answered the LORD and said, "From roaming about on the earth and
walking around on it."

8   The LORD said to Satan, "Have you considered My servant Job? For
there is no one like him on the earth, a blameless and upright man, fearing God and turning away from evil."

9   Then Satan answered the LORD, "Does Job fear God for nothing?

10   "Have You not made a hedge about him and his house and all that
he has, on every side? You have blessed the work of his hands, and his
possessions have increased in the land.

11   "But put forth Your hand now and touch all that he has; he will
surely curse You to Your face."

12   Then the LORD said to Satan, "Behold, all that he has is in your
power, only do not put forth your hand on him." So Satan departed from
the presence of the LORD.

13   Now on the day when his sons and his daughters were eating and
drinking wine in their oldest brother's house,

14   a messenger came to Job and said, "The oxen were plowing and the
donkeys feeding beside them,

15   and the Sabeans attacked and took them. They also slew the servants with the edge of the sword, and I alone have escaped to tell you."

16   While he was still speaking, another also came and said, "The fire of
God fell from heaven and burned up the sheep and the servants and consumed them, and I alone have escaped to tell you."

17   While he was still speaking, another also came and said, "The
Chaldeans formed three bands and made a raid on the camels and took
them and slew the servants with the edge of the sword, and I alone have
escaped to tell you."

18   While he was still speaking, another also came and said, "Your sons and your daughters were eating and drinking wine in their oldest brother's house,

19   and behold, a great wind came from across the wilderness and struck the four corners of the house, and it fell on the young people and they died, and I alone have escaped to tell you."

20   Then Job arose and tore his robe and shaved his head, and he fell to the ground and worshiped.

21   He said,

"Naked I came from my mother's womb,

And naked I shall return there.

The LORD gave and the LORD has taken away.

Blessed be the name of the LORD."

22   Through all this Job did not sin nor did he blame God.

JOB 2

1   Again there was a day when the sons of God came to present themselves before the LORD, and Satan also came among them to present himself before the LORD.

2   The LORD said to Satan, "Where have you come from?" Then Satan answered the LORD and said, "From roaming about on the earth and walking around on it."

3   The LORD said to Satan, "Have you considered My servant Job? For there is no one like him on the earth, a blameless and upright man fearing God and turning away from evil. And he still holds fast his integrity, although you incited Me against him to ruin him without cause."

4   Satan answered the LORD and said, "Skin for skin! Yes, all that a man has he will give for his life.

5   "However, put forth Your hand now, and touch his bone and his flesh; he will curse You to Your face."

6   So the LORD said to Satan, "Behold, he is in your power, only spare his life."

7   Then Satan went out from the presence of the LORD and smote Job with sore boils from the sole of his foot to the crown of his head.

8   And he took a potsherd to scrape himself while he was sitting among the ashes.

9   Then his wife said to him, "Do you still hold fast your integrity? Curse God and die!"

10   But he said to her, "You speak as one of the foolish women speaks. Shall we indeed accept good from God and not accept adversity?" In all this Job did not sin with his lips.

11   Now when Job's three friends heard of all this adversity that had come upon him, they came each one from his own place, Eliphaz the Temanite, Bildad the Shuhite and Zophar the Naamathite; and they made an appointment together to come to sympathize with him and comfort him.

12   When they lifted up their eyes at a distance and did not recognize him, they raised their voices and wept. And each of them tore his robe and they threw dust over their heads toward the sky.

13   Then they sat down on the ground with him for seven days and seven nights with no one speaking a word to him, for they saw that *his* pain was very great.

GENESIS 16

1   Now Sarai, Abram's wife, had borne him no *children,* and she had an Egyptian maid whose name was Hagar.

2   So Sarai said to Abram, "Now behold, the LORD has prevented me from bearing *children.* Please go in to my maid; perhaps I will obtain children through her." And Abram listened to the voice of Sarai.

3   After Abram had lived ten years in the land of Canaan, Abram's wife Sarai took Hagar the Egyptian, her maid, and gave her to her husband Abram as his wife.

4   He went in to Hagar, and she conceived; and when she saw that she had conceived, her mistress was despised in her sight.

5   And Sarai said to Abram, "May the wrong done me be upon you. I gave my maid into your arms, but when she saw that she had conceived, I was despised in her sight. May the LORD judge between you and me."

6   But Abram said to Sarai, "Behold, your maid is in your power; do to her what is good in your sight." So Sarai treated her harshly, and she fled from her presence.

7   Now the angel of the LORD found her by a spring of water in the wilderness, by the spring on the way to Shur.

8   He said, "Hagar, Sarai's maid, where have you come from and where are you going?" And she said, "I am fleeing from the presence of my mistress Sarai."

9   Then the angel of the LORD said to her, "Return to your mistress, and submit yourself to her authority."

10   Moreover, the angel of the LORD said to her, "I will greatly multiply your descendants so that they will be too many to count."

11   The angel of the LORD said to her further,
"Behold, you are with child,
And you will bear a son;
And you shall call his name Ishmael,
Because the LORD has given heed to your affliction.

12   "He will be a wild donkey of a man,
His hand *will be* against everyone,
And everyone's hand *will be* against him;
And he will live to the east of all his brothers."

13   Then she called the name of the LORD who spoke to her, "You are a God who sees"; for she said, "Have I even remained alive here after seeing Him?"

14   Therefore the well was called Beer-lahai-roi; behold, it is between Kadesh and Bered.

15   So Hagar bore Abram a son; and Abram called the name of his son, whom Hagar bore, Ishmael.

16   Abram was eighty-six years old when Hagar bore Ishmael to him.

EXODUS 3

1   Now Moses was pasturing the flock of Jethro his father-in-law, the priest of Midian; and he led the flock to the west side of the wilderness and came to Horeb, the mountain of God.

2   The angel of the LORD appeared to him in a blazing fire from the midst of a bush; and he looked, and behold, the bush was burning with fire, yet the bush was not consumed.

3   So Moses said, "I must turn aside now and see this marvelous sight, why the bush is not burned up."

4   When the LORD saw that he turned aside to look, God called to him from the midst of the bush and said, "Moses, Moses!" And he said, "Here I am."

5   Then He said, "Do not come near here; remove your sandals from your feet, for the place on which you are standing is holy ground."

6   He said also, "I am the God of your father, the God of Abraham, the God of Isaac, and the God of Jacob." Then Moses hid his face, for he was afraid to look at God.

7   The LORD said, "I have surely seen the affliction of My people who are in Egypt, and have given heed to their cry because of their taskmasters, for I am aware of their sufferings.

8   "So I have come down to deliver them from the power of the Egyptians, and to bring them up from that land to a good and spacious land, to a land flowing with milk and honey, to the place of the Canaanite and the Hittite and the Amorite and the Perizzite and the Hivite and the Jebusite.

9   "Now, behold, the cry of the sons of Israel has come to Me; furthermore, I have seen the oppression with which the Egyptians are oppressing them.

10   "Therefore, come now, and I will send you to Pharaoh, so that you may bring My people, the sons of Israel, out of Egypt."

11   But Moses said to God, "Who am I, that I should go to Pharaoh, and that I should bring the sons of Israel out of Egypt?"

12   And He said, "Certainly I will be with you, and this shall be the sign to you that it is I who have sent you: when you have brought the people out of Egypt, you shall worship God at this mountain."

13   Then Moses said to God, "Behold, I am going to the sons of Israel, and I will say to them, 'The God of your fathers has sent me to you.' Now they may say to me, 'What is His name?' What shall I say to them?"

14   God said to Moses, "I AM WHO I AM"; and He said, "Thus you shall say to the sons of Israel, 'I AM has sent me to you.' "

15   God, furthermore, said to Moses, "Thus you shall say to the sons of Israel, 'The LORD, the God of your fathers, the God of Abraham, the God of Isaac, and the God of Jacob, has sent me to you.' This is My name forever, and this is My memorial-name to all generations.

16   "Go and gather the elders of Israel together and say to them, 'The LORD, the God of your fathers, the God of Abraham, Isaac and Jacob, has appeared to me, saying, "I am indeed concerned about you and what has been done to you in Egypt.

17   "So I said, I will bring you up out of the affliction of Egypt to the land of the Canaanite and the Hittite and the Amorite and the Perizzite and the Hivite and the Jebusite, to a land flowing with milk and honey." '

18   "They will pay heed to what you say; and you with the elders of Israel will come to the king of Egypt and you will say to him, 'The LORD, the God of the Hebrews, has met with us. So now, please, let us go a three days' journey into the wilderness, that we may sacrifice to the LORD our God.'

19   "But I know that the king of Egypt will not permit you to go, except under compulsion.

20   "So I will stretch out My hand and strike Egypt with all My miracles which I shall do in the midst of it; and after that he will let you go.

21   "I will grant this people favor in the sight of the Egyptians; and it shall be that when you go, you will not go empty-handed.

22   "But every woman shall ask of her neighbor and the woman who lives in her house, articles of silver and articles of gold, and clothing; and you will put them on your sons and daughters. Thus you will plunder the Egyptians."

GENESIS 22

1   Now it came about after these things, that God tested Abraham, and said to him, "Abraham!" And he said, "Here I am."

2   He said, "Take now your son, your only son, whom you love, Isaac, and go to the land of Moriah, and offer him there as a burnt offering on one of the mountains of which I will tell you."

3   So Abraham rose early in the morning and saddled his donkey, and took two of his young men with him and Isaac his son; and he split wood for the burnt offering, and arose and went to the place of which God had told him.

4   On the third day Abraham raised his eyes and saw the place from a distance.

5   Abraham said to his young men, "Stay here with the donkey, and I and the lad will go over there; and we will worship and return to you."

6   Abraham took the wood of the burnt offering and laid it on Isaac his son, and he took in his hand the fire and the knife. So the two of them walked on together.

7   Isaac spoke to Abraham his father and said, "My father!" And he said, "Here I am, my son." And he said, "Behold, the fire and the wood, but where is the lamb for the burnt offering?"

8   Abraham said, "God will provide for Himself the lamb for the burnt offering, my son." So the two of them walked on together.

9   Then they came to the place of which God had told him; and Abraham built the altar there and arranged the wood, and bound his son Isaac and laid him on the altar, on top of the wood.

10   Abraham stretched out his hand and took the knife to slay his son.

11   But the angel of the LORD called to him from heaven and said, "Abraham, Abraham!" And he said, "Here I am."

12   He said, "Do not stretch out your hand against the lad, and do nothing to him; for now I know that you fear God, since you have not withheld your son, your only son, from Me."

13   Then Abraham raised his eyes and looked, and behold, behind *him* a ram caught in the thicket by his horns; and Abraham went and took the ram and offered him up for a burnt offering in the place of his son.

14   Abraham called the name of that place The LORD Will Provide, as it is said to this day, "In the mount of the LORD it will be provided."

15   Then the angel of the LORD called to Abraham a second time from heaven,

16   and said, "By Myself I have sworn, declares the LORD, because you have done this thing and have not withheld your son, your only son,

17   indeed I will greatly bless you, and I will greatly multiply your seed as the stars of the heavens and as the sand which is on the seashore; and your seed shall possess the gate of their enemies.

18   "In your seed all the nations of the earth shall be blessed, because you have obeyed My voice."

19   So Abraham returned to his young men, and they arose and went together to Beersheba; and Abraham lived at Beersheba.

20   Now it came about after these things, that it was told Abraham, saying, "Behold, Milcah also has borne children to your brother Nahor:

21   Uz his firstborn and Buz his brother and Kemuel the father of Aram

22   and Chesed and Hazo and Pildash and Jidlaph and Bethuel."

23   Bethuel became the father of Rebekah; these eight Milcah bore to Nahor, Abraham's brother.

24   His concubine, whose name was Reumah, also bore Tebah and Gaham and Tahash and Maacah.

EXODUS 17

1   Then all the congregation of the sons of Israel journeyed by stages from the wilderness of Sin, according to the command of the LORD, and camped at Rephidim, and there was no water for the people to drink.

2   Therefore the people quarreled with Moses and said, "Give us water that we may drink." And Moses said to them, "Why do you quarrel with me? Why do you test the LORD?"

3   But the people thirsted there for water; and they grumbled against Moses and said, "Why, now, have you brought us up from Egypt, to kill us and our children and our livestock with thirst?"

4   So Moses cried out to the LORD, saying, "What shall I do to this people? A little more and they will stone me."

5   Then the LORD said to Moses, "Pass before the people and take with you some of the elders of Israel; and take in your hand your staff with which you struck the Nile, and go.

6   "Behold, I will stand before you there on the rock at Horeb; and you shall strike the rock, and water will come out of it, that the people may drink." And Moses did so in the sight of the elders of Israel.

7   He named the place Massah and Meribah because of the quarrel of the sons of Israel, and because they tested the LORD, saying, "Is the LORD among us, or not?"

8   Then Amalek came and fought against Israel at Rephidim.

9   So Moses said to Joshua, "Choose men for us and go out, fight against Amalek. Tomorrow I will station myself on the top of the hill with the staff of God in my hand."

10   Joshua did as Moses told him, and fought against Amalek; and Moses, Aaron, and Hur went up to the top of the hill.

11   So it came about when Moses held his hand up, that Israel prevailed, and when he let his hand down, Amalek prevailed.

12   But Moses' hands were heavy. Then they took a stone and put it under him, and he sat on it; and Aaron and Hur supported his hands, one on one side and one on the other. Thus his hands were steady until the sun set.

13   So Joshua overwhelmed Amalek and his people with the edge of the sword.

14   Then the LORD said to Moses, "Write this in a book as a memorial and recite it to Joshua, that I will utterly blot out the memory of Amalek from under heaven."

15   Moses built an altar and named it The LORD is My Banner;

16   and he said, "The LORD has sworn; the LORD will have war against Amalek from generation to generation."

JUDGES 6

1   Then the sons of Israel did what was evil in the sight of the LORD; and the LORD gave them into the hands of Midian seven years.

2   The power of Midian prevailed against Israel. Because of Midian the sons of Israel made for themselves the dens which were in the mountains and the caves and the strongholds.

3   For it was when Israel had sown, that the Midianites would come up with the Amalekites and the sons of the east and go against them.

4   So they would camp against them and destroy the produce of the earth as far as Gaza, and leave no sustenance in Israel as well as no sheep, ox, or donkey.

5   For they would come up with their livestock and their tents, they would come in like locusts for number, both they and their camels were innumerable; and they came into the land to devastate it.

6   So Israel was brought very low because of Midian, and the sons of Israel cried to the LORD.

7   Now it came about when the sons of Israel cried to the LORD on account of Midian,

8   that the LORD sent a prophet to the sons of Israel, and he said to them, "Thus says the LORD, the God of Israel, 'It was I who brought you up from Egypt and brought you out from the house of slavery.

9   'I delivered you from the hands of the Egyptians and from the hands of all your oppressors, and dispossessed them before you and gave you their land,

10   and I said to you, "I am the LORD your God; you shall not fear the gods of the Amorites in whose land you live. But you have not obeyed Me." ' "

11   Then the angel of the LORD came and sat under the oak that was in Ophrah, which belonged to Joash the Abiezrite as his son Gideon was

beating out wheat in the wine press in order to save *it* from the Midianites.

12   The angel of the LORD appeared to him and said to him, "The LORD is with you, O valiant warrior."

13   Then Gideon said to him, "O my lord, if the LORD is with us, why then has all this happened to us? And where are all His miracles which our fathers told us about, saying, 'Did not the LORD bring us up from Egypt?' But now the LORD has abandoned us and given us into the hand of Midian."

14   The LORD looked at him and said, "Go in this your strength and deliver Israel from the hand of Midian. Have I not sent you?"

15   He said to Him, "O Lord, how shall I deliver Israel? Behold, my family is the least in Manasseh, and I am the youngest in my father's house."

16   But the LORD said to him, "Surely I will be with you, and you shall defeat Midian as one man."

17   So Gideon said to Him, "If now I have found favor in Your sight, then show me a sign that it is You who speak with me.

18   "Please do not depart from here, until I come *back* to You, and bring out my offering and lay it before You." And He said, "I will remain until you return."

19   Then Gideon went in and prepared a young goat and unleavened bread from an ephah of flour; he put the meat in a basket and the broth in a pot, and brought *them* out to him under the oak and presented *them*.

20   The angel of God said to him, "Take the meat and the unleavened bread and lay them on this rock, and pour out the broth." And he did so.

21   Then the angel of the LORD put out the end of the staff that was in his hand and touched the meat and the unleavened bread; and fire sprang up from the rock and consumed the meat and the unleavened bread. Then the angel of the LORD vanished from his sight.

22   When Gideon saw that he was the angel of the LORD, he said, "Alas, O Lord GOD! For now I have seen the angel of the LORD face to face."

23   The LORD said to him, "Peace to you, do not fear; you shall not die."

24   Then Gideon built an altar there to the LORD and named it The LORD is Peace. To this day it is still in Ophrah of the Abiezrites.

25   Now on the same night the LORD said to him, "Take your father's bull and a second bull seven years old, and pull down the altar of Baal which belongs to your father, and cut down the Asherah that is beside it;

26   and build an altar to the LORD your God on the top of this strong- hold in an orderly manner, and take a second bull and offer a burnt offer- ing with the wood of the Asherah which you shall cut down."

27   Then Gideon took ten men of his servants and did as the LORD had spoken to him; and because he was too afraid of his father's household and the men of the city to do it by day, he did it by night.

28   When the men of the city arose early in the morning, behold, the altar of Baal was torn down, and the Asherah which was beside it was cut down, and the second bull was offered on the altar which had been built.

29   They said to one another, "Who did this thing?" And when they searched about and inquired, they said, "Gideon the son of Joash did this thing."

30   Then the men of the city said to Joash, "Bring out your son, that he may die, for he has torn down the altar of Baal, and indeed, he has cut down the Asherah which was beside it."

31   But Joash said to all who stood against him, "Will you contend for Baal, or will you deliver him? Whoever will plead for him shall be put to death by morning. If he is a god, let him contend for himself, because someone has torn down his altar."

32   Therefore on that day he named him Jerubbaal, that is to say, "Let Baal contend against him," because he had torn down his altar.

33   Then all the Midianites and the Amalekites and the sons of the east assembled themselves; and they crossed over and camped in the valley of Jezreel.

34   So the Spirit of the LORD came upon Gideon; and he blew a trumpet, and the Abiezrites were called together to follow him.

35   He sent messengers throughout Manasseh, and they also were called together to follow him; and he sent messengers to Asher, Zebulun, and Naphtali, and they came up to meet them.

36   Then Gideon said to God, "If You will deliver Israel through me, as You have spoken,

37   behold, I will put a fleece of wool on the threshing floor. If there is dew on the fleece only, and it is dry on all the ground, then I will know that You will deliver Israel through me, as You have spoken."

38   And it was so. When he arose early the next morning and squeezed the fleece, he drained the dew from the fleece, a bowl full of water.

39   Then Gideon said to God, "Do not let Your anger burn against me that I may speak once more; please let me make a test once more with the fleece, let it now be dry only on the fleece, and let there be dew on all the ground."

40   God did so that night; for it was dry only on the fleece, and dew was on all the ground.

JOHN 10

1   "Truly, truly, I say to you, he who does not enter by the door into the fold of the sheep, but climbs up some other way, he is a thief and a robber.

2   "But he who enters by the door is a shepherd of the sheep.

3   "To him the doorkeeper opens, and the sheep hear his voice, and he calls his own sheep by name and leads them out.

4   "When he puts forth all his own, he goes ahead of them, and the sheep follow him because they know his voice.

5   "A stranger they simply will not follow, but will flee from him, because they do not know the voice of strangers."

6   This figure of speech Jesus spoke to them, but they did not understand what those things were which He had been saying to them.

7   So Jesus said to them again, "Truly, truly, I say to you, I am the door of the sheep.

8   "All who came before Me are thieves and robbers, but the sheep did not hear them.

9   "I am the door; if anyone enters through Me, he will be saved, and will go in and out and find pasture.

10   "The thief comes only to steal and kill and destroy; I came that they may have life, and have *it* abundantly.

11   "I am the good shepherd; the good shepherd lays down His life for the sheep.

12   "He who is a hired hand, and not a shepherd, who is not the owner of the sheep, sees the wolf coming, and leaves the sheep and flees, and the wolf snatches them and scatters *them*.

13   "*He flees* because he is a hired hand and is not concerned about the sheep.

14   "I am the good shepherd, and I know My own and My own know Me,

15   even as the Father knows Me and I know the Father; and I lay down My life for the sheep.

16   "I have other sheep, which are not of this fold; I must bring them also, and they will hear My voice; and they will become one flock *with* one shepherd.

17   "For this reason the Father loves Me, because I lay down My life so that I may take it again.

18   "No one has taken it away from Me, but I lay it down on My own initiative. I have authority to lay it down, and I have authority to take it up again. This commandment I received from My Father."

19   A division occurred again among the Jews because of these words.

20   Many of them were saying, "He has a demon and is insane. Why do you listen to Him?"

21   Others were saying, "These are not the sayings of one demon-possessed. A demon cannot open the eyes of the blind, can he?"

22   At that time the Feast of the Dedication took place at Jerusalem;

23   it was winter, and Jesus was walking in the temple in the portico of Solomon.

24   The Jews then gathered around Him, and were saying to Him, "How long will You keep us in suspense? If You are the Christ, tell us plainly."

25   Jesus answered them, "I told you, and you do not believe; the works that I do in My Father's name, these testify of Me.

26   "But you do not believe because you are not of My sheep.

27   "My sheep hear My voice, and I know them, and they follow Me;

28   and I give eternal life to them, and they will never perish; and no one will snatch them out of My hand.

29   "My Father, who has given *them* to Me, is greater than all; and no one is able to snatch *them* out of the Father's hand.

30   "I and the Father are one."

31   The Jews picked up stones again to stone Him.

32   Jesus answered them, "I showed you many good works from the Father; for which of them are you stoning Me?"

33   The Jews answered Him, "For a good work we do not stone You, but for blasphemy; and because You, being a man, make Yourself out *to be* God."

34   Jesus answered them, "Has it not been written in your Law, 'I SAID, YOU ARE GODS'?

35   "If he called them gods, to whom the word of God came (and the Scripture cannot be broken),

36   do you say of Him, whom the Father sanctified and sent into the world, 'You are blaspheming,' because I said, 'I am the Son of God'?

37   "If I do not do the works of My Father, do not believe Me;

38 · but if I do them, though you do not believe Me, believe the works, so that you may know and understand that the Father is in Me, and I in the Father."

39   Therefore they were seeking again to seize Him, and He eluded their grasp.

40   And He went away again beyond the Jordan to the place where John was first baptizing, and He was staying there.

41   Many came to Him and were saying, "While John performed no sign, yet everything John said about this man was true."

42   Many believed in Him there.